MEND YOUR WAY TO Sustainable Style

Cosabeth Parriaud

Landauer Publishing

Mend Your Way to Sustainable Style

Mend Your Way to Sustainable Style is a translation of the original French book published by Éditions Marie Claire under the title *Atelier couture, lifting pour mon dressing*. This version published by Landauer Publishing, www.landauer.foxchapelpublishing.com, an imprint of Fox Chapel Publishing Company, Inc.

Project Team
Editorial Director: Brian Hurley
Acquisitions Editor: Amelia Johanson
Editor: Christa Oestreich
Designer: Leslie Hall

ISBN 978-1-63981-156-4

Library of Congress Control Number: 2025950069

To learn more about the other great books from Fox Chapel Publishing, or to find a retailer near you, call toll-free at 800-457-9112 or visit us at www.FoxChapelPublishing.com.
We are always looking for talented authors.
To submit an idea, please send a brief inquiry to acquisitions@foxchapelpublishing.com.
Or write to:
Fox Chapel Publishing
903 Square Street
Mount Joy, PA 17552

Printed in China
First printing

FOREWORD

In an age when efforts are being made to reduce waste and clutter, how about recycling or upcycling your clothes? Because the textile industry is one of the biggest polluters in the world, it's time to go green and take a stand against fast fashion.

In the past, mending and repairing were done as discreetly as possible; today, we embrace and showcase them! Hide a stain or hole with some embroidery or pretty fabric, lengthen pants that are too short, spruce up a faded shirt, give a sweater a new look, or personalize a T-shirt—the possibilities are endless! This way, you can keep wearing the clothes you love, and they become even more special because of all the time you've spent fixing them up. These activities can also be therapeutic. When you're focused on a sewing project, you forget about stress. And when you do it with friends, you get to share some great creative memories.

Everyone can do these projects! You don't need to be an expert sewist to get started. There are some very simple techniques, and the basic equipment doesn't cost an arm and a leg. All you really need: a sewing kit, a few scraps of fabric, and some clothing items. You're ready to roll!

Templates are used throughout the book to achieve the exact look of each design. While some are presented at actual size, others will need to be enlarged when photocopied and printed. A percentage is given for each relevant pattern. You can also download the full-size template files by scanning the QR code or going to the following website: https://foxpatterns.com/sewing-workshop-wardrobe-makeover

CONTENTS

TOOLS AND MATERIALS

FABRIC

Many fabrics are suitable for the designs in this book. I used fabrics made of cotton, wool, and upholstery fabrics as well as old jeans and sweaters.

With some exceptions, quantities are not specified in the materials list, as the idea is to use up any scraps and small pieces of fabric you already have at home. Be sure to choose scraps that are wide enough, though. That way, you'll have enough extra fabric should you make a mistake when cutting.

- **Cotton:** This type of fabric generally has a width of 43" (109.2cm), unlike most other fabrics, which are 55" (139.7cm) wide. Choose high-quality 100% cotton fabrics. Wash and iron before use. This will help prevent any future shrinkage. It will also allow you to check that the color does not run. If it does, rinse the fabric several times. If there is still color in the water, soak your fabric for one hour in a solution of two parts water and one part white vinegar. Rinse thoroughly. If the color continues to run, don't use it—unless it is paired with dark fabrics, in which case, it won't be a problem when washed in the future.
- **Wool:** You'll find these fabrics sold by the yard in fabric stores or by hunting for old tweed clothing at yard sales.
- **Upholstery fabrics:** These are heavier than cotton but are very easy to use.
- **Denim:** Recycling your old jeans prevents waste and provides you with a beautiful palette of various shades of blue.
- **Old sweaters:** When they're worn out or have holes in them, adding onto your sweaters is great way to recycle them. To prevent the stitches from unraveling when assembling appliqué patchwork pieces, you can press iron-on adhesive to the wrong side before sewing.

SEWING MACHINE

A domestic sewing machine can be used to put together all the designs in this book. However, make sure that it has good feed-through and includes a few stretchy stitches, such as the stretch stitch or zigzag stitch, which will allow you to sew on fabrics that give. Leading brands offer sewing machine models specifically designed for patchwork, so don't hesitate to ask for advice in store.

Don't forget to clean and oil your machine regularly! Also be sure to choose the right sewing needle for your fabric.

You will also need several types of presser feet:

- A **patchwork foot** for precise quilting to ⅜" (1cm) from the edge.
- A **special foot** for denim and layers.
- A **dual-feed/walking presser foot** (optional). This foot is perfect for sewing strips or quilting, as it feeds the different thicknesses of the top and bottom layers at the same speed.

UPHOLSTERY FABRIC
WOOL FABRIC
COTTON FABRIC IN PRINTS
TAPE MEASURE
MARKING PENCILS
STRAIGHT RULER
STRAIGHT PINS
COTTON FABRIC IN SOLIDS
SEAM RIPPER
HAND SEWING NEEDLES
DENIM
SPOOLS OF THREAD
THREAD SNIPS
FABRIC SCISSORS

TOOLS AND NOTIONS

- **Thread:** Choose good-quality thread to avoid the fluff that can clog your machine. Gütermann's polyester series is ideal, as is the thread made by Mettler. You can also use 40 or 50 wt. cotton thread.
- **Long, straight pins:** These are used to hold layers of fabric together before you stitch.
- **Tape measure:** I prefer a dressmaker's tape measure rather than the stiff one used for carpentry.
- **Sewing scissors:** You'll need several pairs: one large pair and one small pair with pointed tips. Only use them to cut fabric. Never cut paper or any other material, as this will dull the blades.
- **Ruler:** Used for tracing sewing lines.
- **Marking pencils:** After making a line on the fabric, this mark can be erased with water or an iron, depending on the type of marking tool. You can buy them from craft and fabric suppliers.
- **Tailor's chalk or a chalk roller:** Use to draw fine lines on dark or wool fabrics. These marks will wipe away to the touch.
- **Heat-erasable fabric pen:** Used similarly to marking pencils, my favorite is the Pilot FriXion pen.
- **Water-soluble felt pen:** Use for transferring patterns onto light- or medium-colored fabrics. The line can be removed with a little water. Be careful not to iron over the design, as the heat may cause the marks to become permanent.
- **Seam ripper:** Used when you make a mistake in your stitching.
- **Double-sided iron-on interfacing:** It comes in different thicknesses to suit the type of fabric. I use Vliesofix Bondaweb™.
- **Iron-on interfacing.** Used to add stability and strength to fabric. It adheres with heat and is permanent.
- **Pencil:** I suggest well-sharpened or mechanical pencil for thin lines.
- **Square ruler:** These are typically clear, making it easy to see the fabric below while you cut along the edges.
- **Acetate sheets:** Available in specialty stores, transparent acetate sheets are used to make templates. Failing that, use lightweight cardboard.
- **Cardstock:** This thick paper is another option for making templates.

For embroidery:

- **Pearl cotton thread or other embroidery threads:** I recommend getting size 8 thread in various colors.
- **Embroidery needles:** There are a variety of options out there, but picking hand sewing needles mostly comes down to personal preference.

PIECING

A LITTLE HISTORY

Whenever someone thinks of a "quilt," what they picture is typically just one style, called "patchwork." While patchwork is the most traditional design, there are many quilt designs, and the techniques for making them—called "piecing"—is the same! It consists of joining together bits of fabric in different sizes and colors. To make a quilt, the whole thing is then lined and filled with batting, which is then secured in place with stitches, a technique known as "quilting."

These techniques have a very long history. Traces have been found in India and Egypt. European settlers brought the tradition with them to the New World when they crossed the Atlantic. Quilts are often made using patchwork blocks, which are patterns made up of several small pieces of different shapes, such as squares, triangles, rectangles, and diamonds. It's a great way to recycle small scraps of fabric that you would otherwise throw away.

Quilting developed more widely in the United States, where it became a popular art form in its own right. With the Industrial Revolution, the availability of cheap cotton fabrics completely changed the tradition. Quilting was no longer just a practical activity; American women bought fabric specifically to make their quilts.

The appliqué technique also developed, which is typically used with rounded shapes. By the 1940s, though, the tradition was running out of steam.

It was then revived in the 1960s when quilts were recognized for their artistic value. In 1971, the first exhibition was held at the Whitney Museum in New York. In 1972, the Musée des Arts Décoratifs in Paris hosted an exhibition, attracting huge interest and inspiring many people in Europe, Japan, and Australia to take up the craft.

Nowadays, encouraged by the trend toward reuse and recycling, the art of patchwork and quilting is enjoying a new lease of life.

HOW TO

PREPARING THE TEMPLATE

The templates for various shapes provided in this book include seam allowances (unless otherwise indicated). All pieces must therefore be cut to include this seam allowance. It's about ¼" (6.4mm) on all sides.

For example, if you need a finished (i.e., sewn) 2" x 2" (5.1 x 5.1cm) square, you'll need to cut a 2½" x 2½" (6.4 x 6.4cm) square.

1 Trace the templates onto a sheet of acetate, cardstock paper, or a lightweight piece of cardboard. The key is that the template is sturdy enough, but not too thick.

2 Cut along the lines.

FABRIC DIRECTION

To prevent fabric distortion during assembly, the grain line must run along the edge of the pieces.

3 For triangular pieces, place the grain along one of the edges, forming a right angle. Exception: When the triangle's diagonal edge will be outside the block. In this case, the diagonal must be in line with the grain.

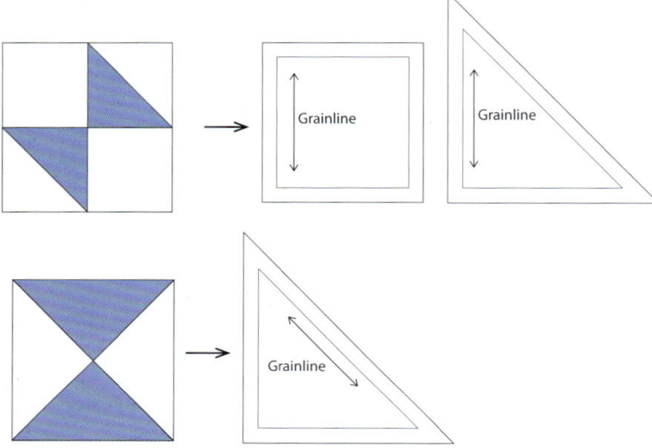

CUTTING THE TEMPLATE

4 Place the acetate or cardboard template on the wrong side of the fabric.

5 Using a pencil, trace around the templates. Cut out the fabric along the outline.

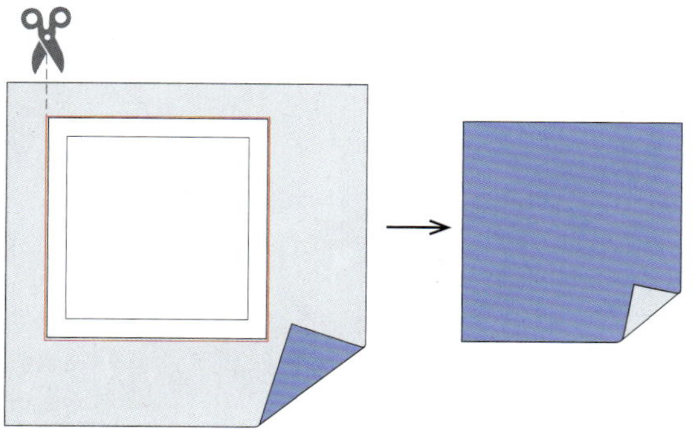

ASSEMBLING

6 Choose a thread that matches the dominant colors for the spool and a neutral thread for the bobbin.

7 It's really important to be precise when assembling to ensure the seam allowance is the same throughout. Always sew ¼" (6.4mm) from the edge, meaning your presser foot should be flush with the edge of your fabric.

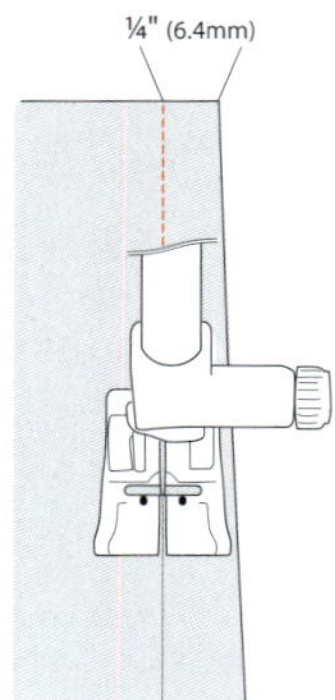

8 When assembling a half-square triangle, after pressing the seam allowances, cut off the tails that stick out at the ends.

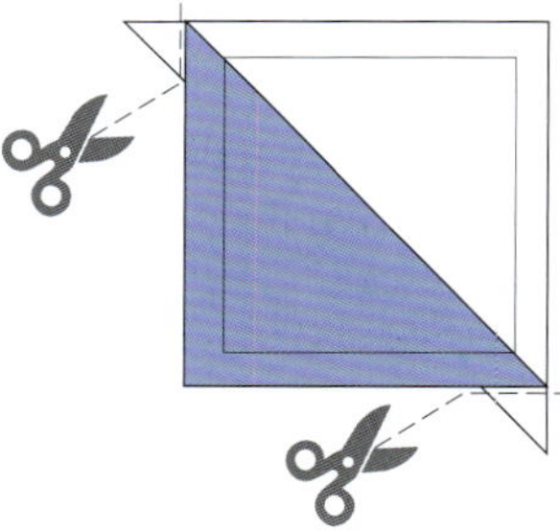

9 To assemble strips that are made of several units, place the two strips right sides together, aligning the seams and matching the seam allowances. Pin perpendicular to the edge of the fabric, first at the aligned seams, then at each end.

10 When sewing, there is no need to reverse stitch. You can leave the pins in and only remove them at the end, unless they get in the way. In that case, remove them as you go. Cut the threads at the top and bottom of the seam, leaving only ⅜" (1cm).

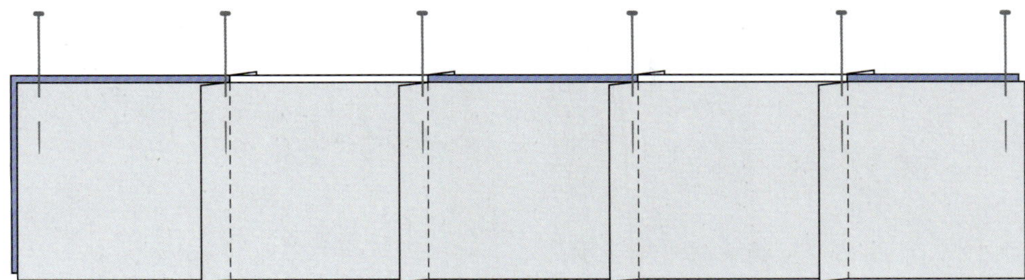

CREATING PERFECT CORNERS

Piecing is like a jigsaw puzzle—once the pieces are assembled, they have to fit together perfectly. Unlike a jigsaw puzzle, however, the pieces of patchwork have a seam allowance. If seam allowances are not consistent, you may experience problems joining the pieces together.

EXAMPLES OF COMMON PROBLEMS

- **The four squares are not aligned.** If this happens, seam rip the stitching. Pin it and then stitch the seams together again.

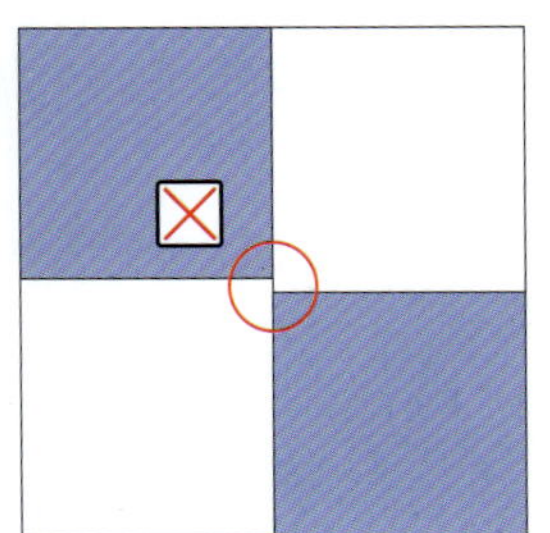

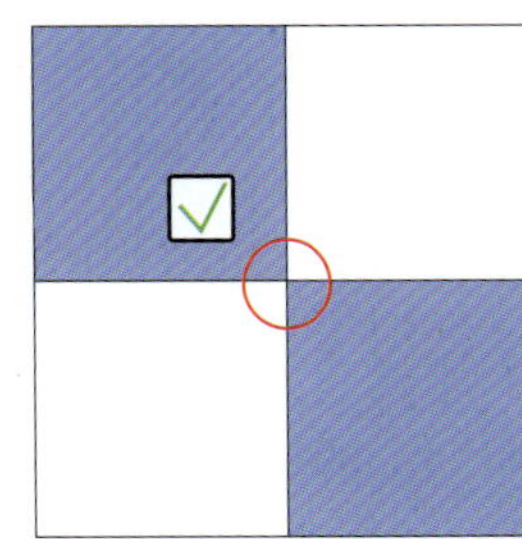

- **The half-square triangle is too small to fit the other units.** Check your seam allowance. If it is more than ¼" (6.4mm), undo it and stitch again exactly ¼" (6.4mm) from the edge.

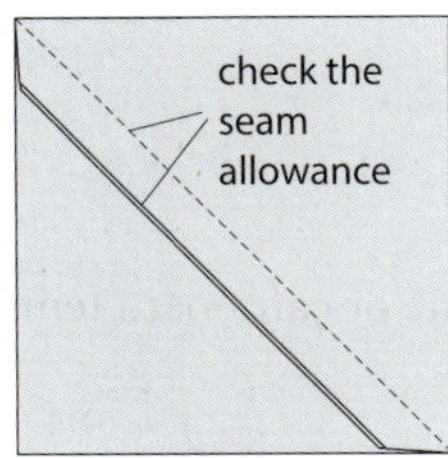

PRESSING

11 Smooth out the seams with your fingernail to avoid unwanted creases. Then go over them lightly with an iron.

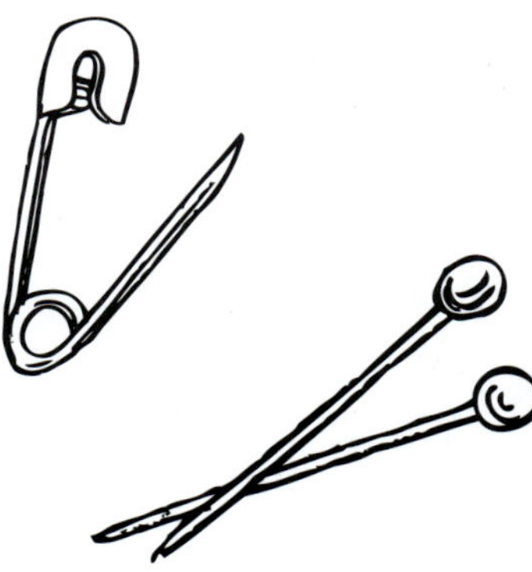

CRAZY QUILT

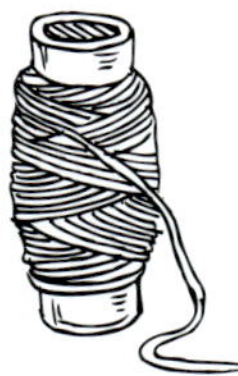

The crazy quilt technique involves sewing pieces of fabric of irregular shapes and sizes together in an asymmetrical pattern. It was all the rage during the Victorian era, when it was usually produced in velvet and silk with the entire surface embroidered.

This technique is done on iron-on interfacing and allows you to use up all your scraps. Thin fabrics like cotton are best, as wool and velvet are too thick and won't stick well.

HOW TO

1 Draw the shape you want on the iron-on interfacing. Cut ⅜" (1cm) around the edge. To avoid confusion, redraw the outline on the other side of the piece of interfacing (the shiny side with the adhesive).

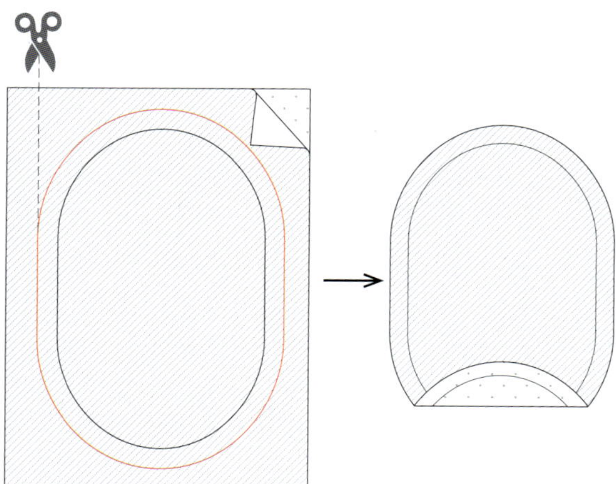

2 Arrange small pieces of fabric in different colors on the adhesive side of the shape. Make sure that the pieces overlap slightly and that they extend beyond the outline of the shape.

3 Once you have arranged your design, press with a hot iron to activate the adhesive and secure the pieces of fabric.

4 If you haven't completely covered the interfacing, place a damp cloth or piece of fabric over it before ironing to prevent the adhesive from sticking to the iron.

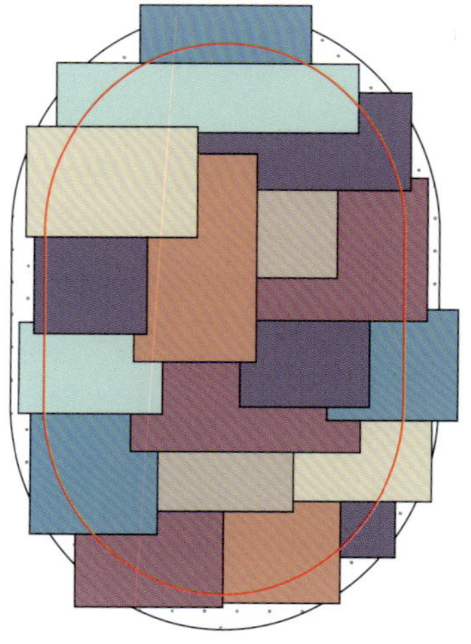

5 To finish securing your fabric scraps, embroider each piece using a running stitch or a decorative embroidery stitch (see pages 20–21) using different thread colors. Be careful to start and finish your stitches inside the outline.

6 Cut out the shape following the outline, taking care not to cut the embroidery threads that start and end the stitches.

YO-YO TECHNIQUE

In terms of quilting, yo-yos are small circles of gathered fabric that make pretty, decorative elements. They are used in the Jacket with Yo-Yos (page 92).

Yo-yos are best made with fairly thin fabrics, such as cotton or silk. Avoid large patterns, which won't look good once the circle is gathered; go for fabrics with small prints, small checks, thin stripes, textured single colors, and solids.

HOW TO

1 Trace the circle template onto an acetate sheet or cardboard. Cut along the lines. Place the template on the wrong side of the fabric, trace around it, then cut out the fabric circle.

2 Thread a needle with a matching-color thread. Tie a double knot at the end, leaving ¼" (6.4mm) of thread beyond the knot.

3 With the wrong side of the fabric circle facing you, fold the edge ¼" (6.4mm) inward. Sew large running stitches (see page 20) close to the fold. Do not backstitch.

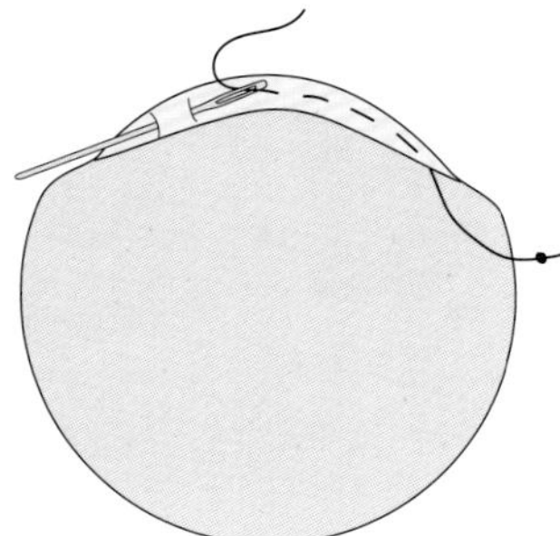

4 When you get back to where you started sewing, gently pull the thread to gather the circle as much as possible. Be careful not to break the thread. Tie the two thread ends securely together.

5 Don't cut the threads, but tuck them inside the yo-yo. Flatten the circle to shape the yo-yo and distribute the gathers evenly.

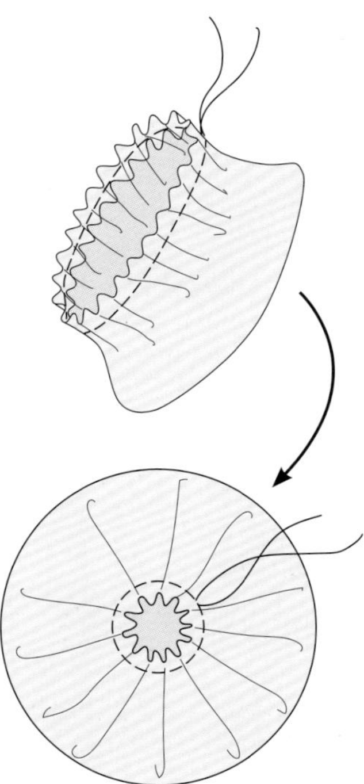

6 If you want to make larger or smaller yo-yos than those shown, draw new circles, keeping in mind the proportions.

BORO

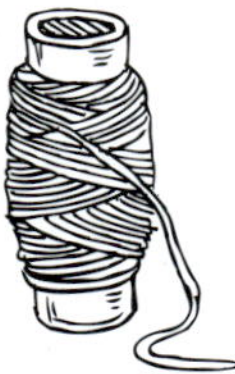

Boro is a Japanese word, meaning "torn rags." This technique for patching fabric dates back to the 17th century and was used up until the mid-20th century, mainly in northern Japan. Poor fishermen and farmers would salvage and recycle even the smallest scraps of fabric to repair and mend their clothes and bedding. They put these little pieces on top of each other and held them in place with stitches.

This practice was mainly carried out with hemp, before cotton became an affordable fabric. The predominant color was indigo blue, with occasional brown tones. These garments were passed down from one generation to the next, and only a few examples, now considered works of art, have survived.

This traditional craft has long since disappeared in Japan, but thanks to the upcycling trend, it is enjoying a revival in the world of patchwork. Using old jeans is reminiscent of the indigo used in days gone by, but you can also choose other types of fabric, such as wool, cotton, linen, plain or printed fabrics, and a variety of colors.

SEE THE TUTORIAL ON PAGE 95.

TRADITIONAL APPLIQUÉ

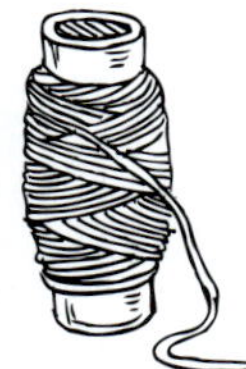

This technique, also called "turned-edge appliqué," involves sewing different pieces of fabric onto a background. It's mainly used for shapes with rounded edges, such as flowers, circles, etc., but it also works really well for geometric shapes like squares and rectangles.

HOW TO

PREPARING THE TEMPLATE

1 Trace the template outline without seam allowances onto an acetate sheet or cardboard, and cut along the lines.

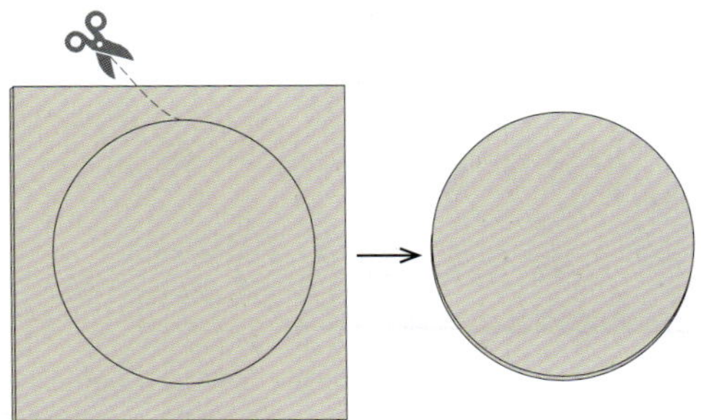

2 Place the template on the wrong side of your chosen fabric. If there are several, space them apart.

3 Cut around, adding a ¼" (6.4mm) seam allowance.

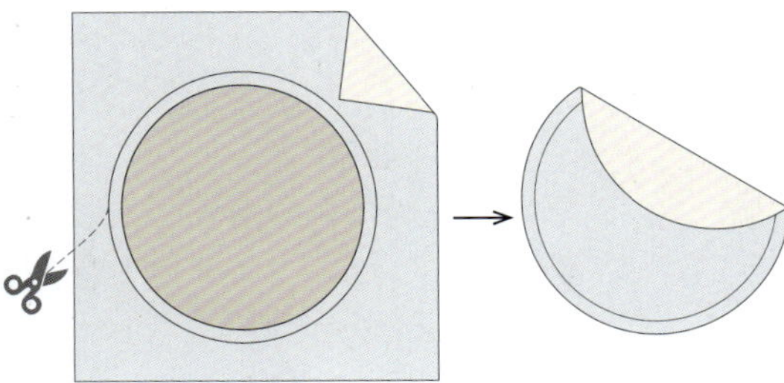

TURNING THE EDGES

4 Fold a piece of fabric twice, creating four layers. This little "mat" will be thick enough for the next step. Place the shape right side down on top of the mat.

5 Using the tip of a straight pin or a safety pin, redraw the shape ¼" (6.4mm) from the edge by pressing well to form small indents. This will simplify the assembly stage.

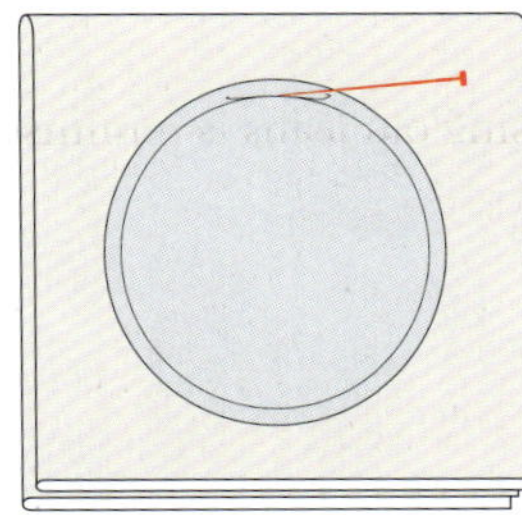

6 Clip all around the seam allowance of the rounded shapes, going to about ⅛" (3.2mm) from the line.

7 For concave shapes, clip to about 1⁄16" (1.6mm) from the line.

8 Fold all the "tabs" of the seam allowance over to the wrong side of the fabric, using the line marked earlier with the pin. Baste in place.

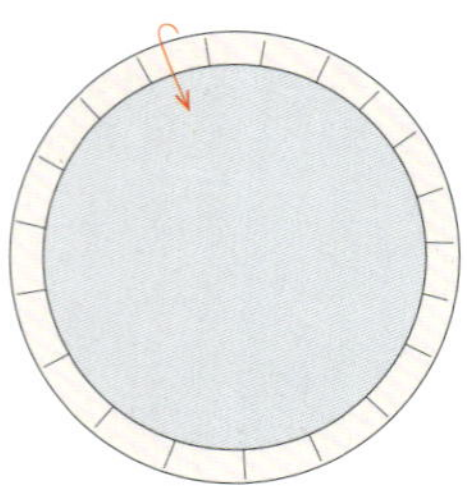

9 For pointed ends, follow these steps: Cut the tip to within ¼" (6.4mm) of the line. Fold down the seam allowance at the tip. Fold down the right side then the left side.

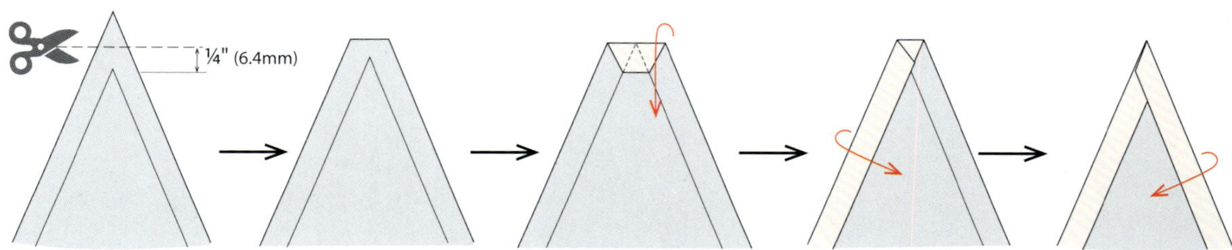

ATTACHING THE SHAPES

10 Position the shapes on the right side of the base fabric, and baste around the edges. Sew on using small slip stitches in a matching thread. Remove the basting stitches.

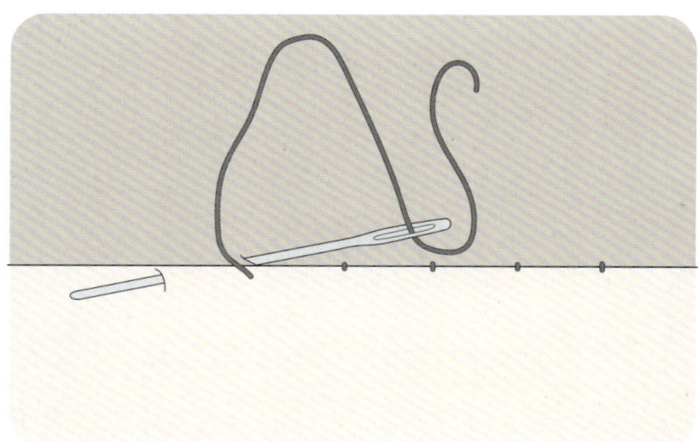

SEE THE TUTORIAL ON PAGE 88.

RAW-EDGE APPLIQUÉ

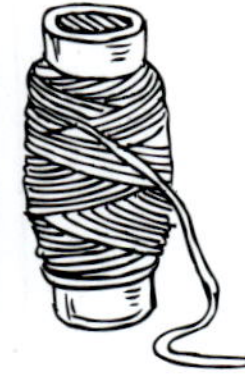

This technique involves attaching pieces of fabric to the base just as they are. Unlike traditional appliqué, the edges are not turned. The pieces are positioned and basted, then sewn on using whichever stitch you prefer (see pages 20–21).

Avoid thick or loose-knit fabrics, as they may fray.

SEE THE TUTORIAL ON PAGE 50.

SEE THE TUTORIAL ON PAGE 65.

REVERSE APPLIQUÉ

Reverse appliqué involves attaching a shape to the wrong side of the fabric. In this method, you cut out the desired shape in the base fabric, then place another piece of fabric underneath the cutout. This avoids additional layers.

HOW TO

1 Draw the desired shape on the right side of your base fabric. Carefully cut along the lines so that the inside of the shape is removed.

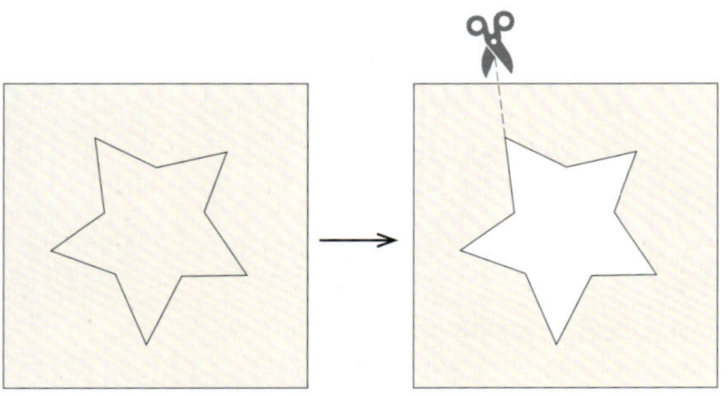

2 Place another piece of fabric behind the base fabric, aligning it with the cutout; both should be right side up. The second fabric should be at least ¾" (1.9cm) larger all around the cutout shape. Pin, then baste close to the edge. Sew through both layers of fabric using any stitch you like (see pages 20–21).

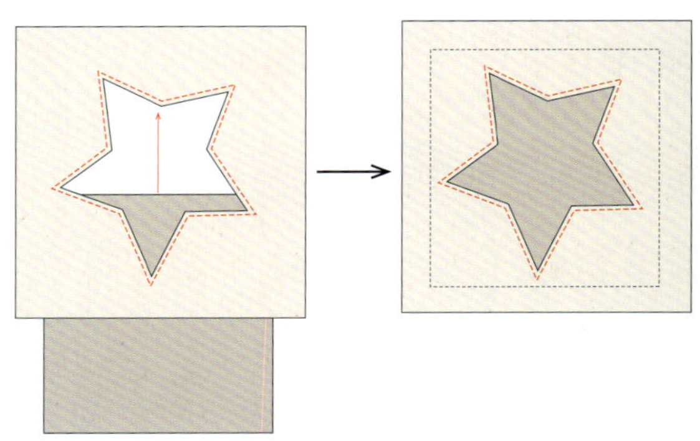

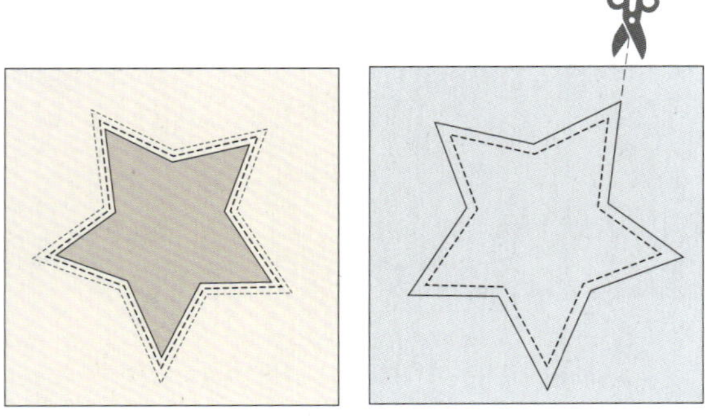

3 Remove the basting thread, then cut the bottom fabric to ⅜" (1cm) all around the cutout shape.

IRON-ON APPLIQUÉ

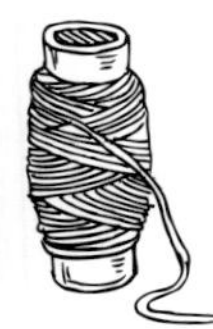

This technique involves gluing a pattern onto the base fabric using double-sided iron-on interfacing. To secure the shape, it's best to sew around it by hand or with a sewing machine.

This ancient appliqué technique, which was very popular in Europe in the 17th century, probably originated in India. It is used for the women's shirt on page 48.

HOW TO

1 Draw the outline of your chosen shape onto the backing sheet of the iron-on interfacing. If the template is not symmetrical, turn it around so that it is reversed.

2 Cut around the outline, ¼" (6.4mm) from the line.

3 Place the adhesive side of the shape on the wrong side of your fabric. Press for a few seconds with a hot iron (no steam) to make the adhesive stick.

4 Cut out the paper and fabric, following the outline of the shape.

5 Remove the backing paper.

6 Place the second adhesive side of the shape onto the right side of your base fabric and iron for a few seconds to secure. Sew small stitches all around, or use a decorative embroidery stitch (see pages 20–21).

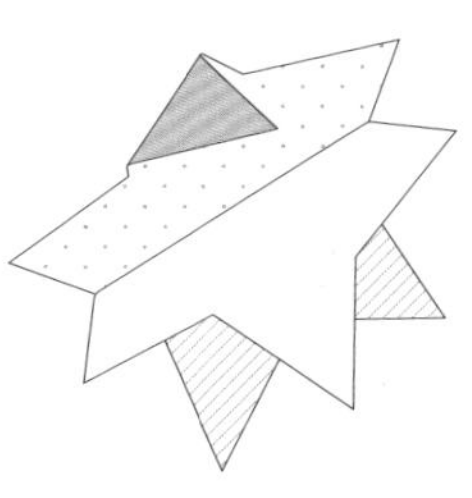

EMBROIDERY

To get started, you will need embroidery needles and embroidery thread. I recommend pearl cotton in size 8 or 5, but you can use any other thread you like.

Here are the main embroidery stitches used for the designs in this book.

HOW TO

RUNNING STITCH

This stitch is used to embroider straight or curved lines.

1 Bring the needle out at point **A** on the right side of the fabric.

2 Insert the needle through the fabric at point **B** and bring it back up a short distance away at point **C**.

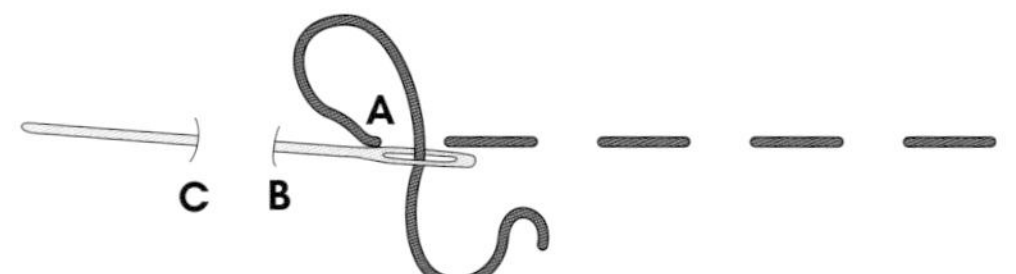

STRAIGHT STITCH

When used in embroidery, the straight stitch can create a series of lines. It's best to do this using two parallel lines to get an even stitch.

1 Bring the needle out at point **A** on the right side of the fabric, on Line 1.

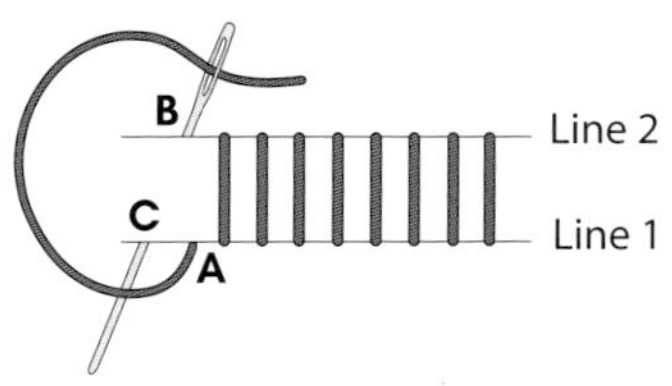

2 Insert the needle through the fabric at point **B** on Line 2, keeping it parallel, then bring it out diagonally at point **C** on Line 1.

3 Repeat steps 1 and 2 as many times as necessary.

BLANKET STITCH

This stitch is used to decorate and finish edges, and to attach pieces of fabric to a textile base. It is also the basis for many other stitches. The technique works from left to right.

1 Insert the needle at point **A** on the right side of the fabric.

2 Insert the needle at point **B** on the underside of the fabric, and bring it out at point **C**. Make sure that when the needle comes out at point **C**, it passes over the loop of thread. Pull the thread tight to form the stitch.

3 Repeat steps 1 and 2 as many times as necessary. The tension must remain the same in each stitch.

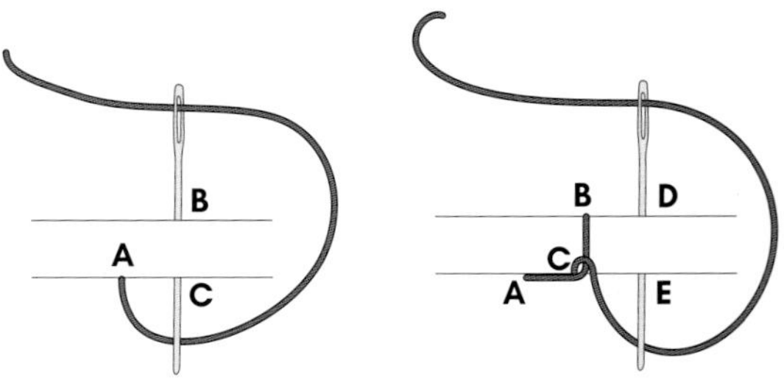

CROSS-STITCH

Each cross-stitch should be the same size and at the same angle. This means working across two parallel lines.

These instructions detail how to make several successive cross-stitches. You can also make isolated cross-stitches using the same technique.

1 Bring the needle out at point **A** on the right side of the fabric, on Line 1.

2 Insert the needle at point **B** diagonally on Line 2, through to the underside of the fabric.

3 Bring it out at point **C** on Line 1, parallel to point **B**.

4 Repeat steps 1–3 for as many cross-stitches as you need.

5 Reverse the process, inserting the needle into the same holes as before.

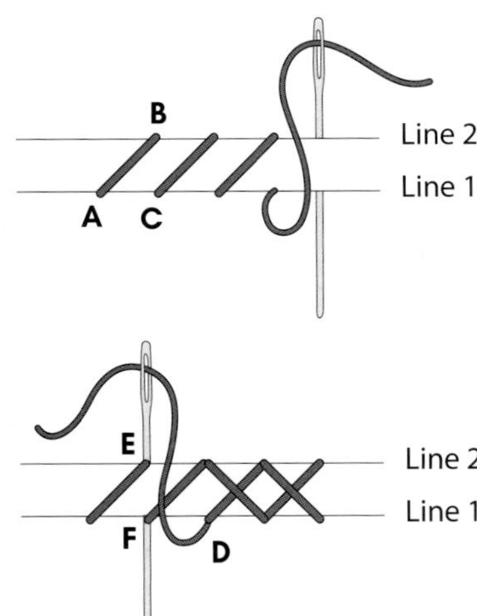

STAR STITCH

1 Bring the needle out at point **A** on the right side of the fabric, at the tip of one of the points of the star.

2 Insert the needle through to the underside of the fabric at point **B**, which will be the center of the star.

3 Bring it out again at point **C**, the tip of the next point.

4 Insert it again at point **B** in the center, and bring it out at point **D**.

5 Continue like this until your star is complete. Make sure you always insert your needle back into the same central point.

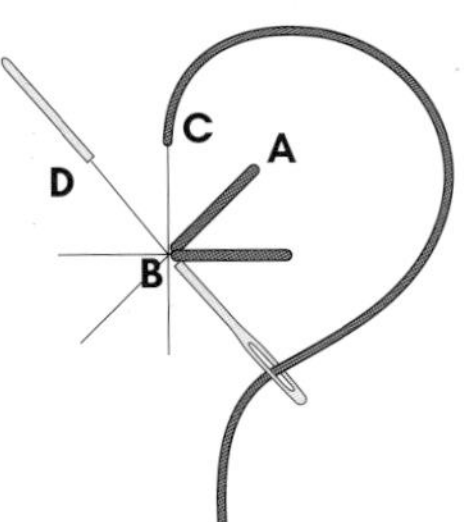

FRENCH KNOT

1 Bring the needle out at point **A** on the right side of the fabric.

2 Hold the thread between your left thumb and index finger, and wrap it around the needle once or twice.

3 Without letting go of the thread, insert the needle through to the underside again at point **A**. Pull the thread enough to position the loops flat against the fabric.

4 To make another knot, continue by inserting the needle at point **B** (at the desired distance from point **A**) on the right side of the fabric, and repeat the previous steps.

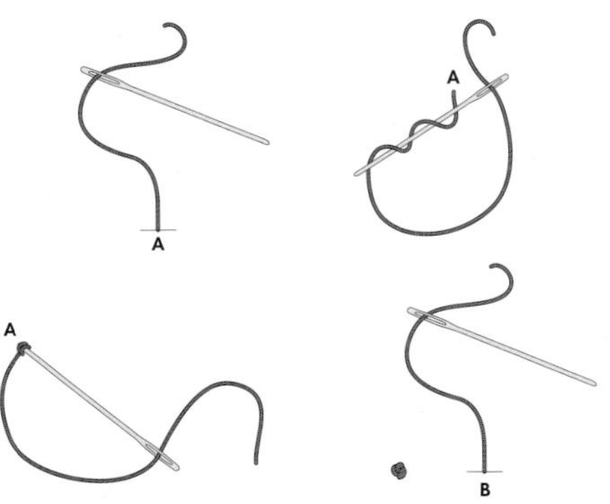

THE PROJECTS

Dresden Plate T-Shirt

TECHNIQUES
- Piecing and traditional appliqué
- *See pages 9 and 15.*

MATERIALS
- Acetate sheet
- Scraps of solid fabric
- Matching threads
- T-shirt

This Dresden Plate design is a classic American quilting block, particularly popular from the 1930s onward. It resembles the traditional porcelain plates produced in Dresden, Germany. It's a good bet that this design was brought over by German immigrants when they came to the New World.

1 Using the sheet of acetate, mark and cut out the templates for petal A and circle B (see page 27).

2 Trace Template A onto the wrong side of 12 different pieces of fabric and cut around the outlines.

3 Join six petals for one half of the Dresden Plate. At the top of each petal, leave ¼" (6.4mm) unsewn (this will make it easier to baste the outer edge of the Plate before fixing it in place). Iron all the seam allowances in the same direction.

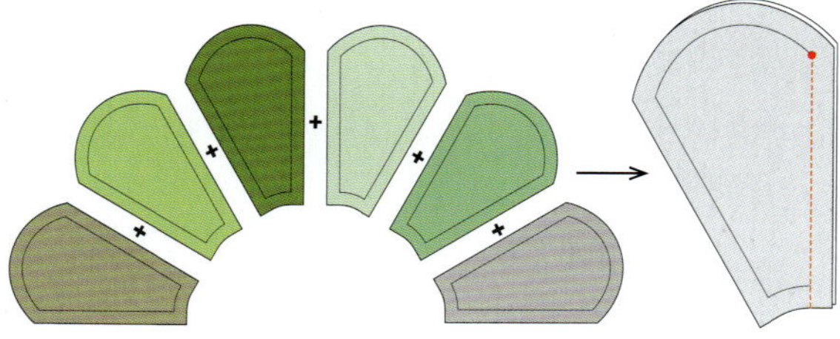

4 Assemble the other half (the six remaining petals) in the same way, then join the two halves using the same technique.

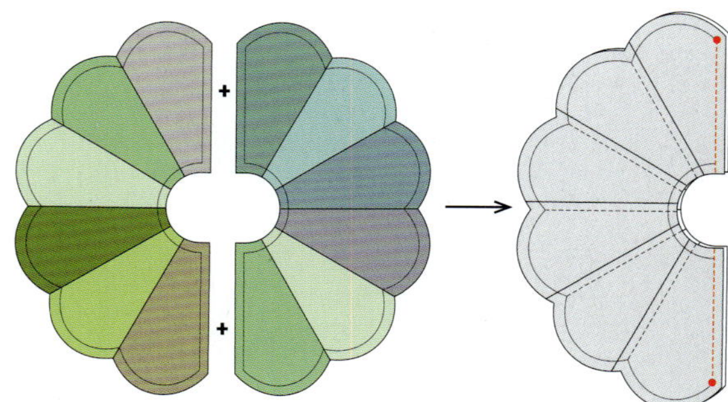

5 Every ⅜" (1cm), clip the rounded outer part to a depth of ⅛" (3.2mm). Fold the tabs of the ¼" (6.4mm) seam allowance and baste the edge. Take your time to ensure that the curves are even.

DANIEL PENNAC
nrf

6 Trace Template B onto a contrasting piece of fabric. Cut out, adding a ¼" (6.4mm) seam allowance all around the outline. Clip and baste using the traditional appliqué technique (page 15).

7 Position the Plate on the T-shirt, making sure it's centered, then baste. Sew around the outer edge using small slip stitches.

8 Place the circle in the center, covering the Plate's seam allowances. Pin, baste, and sew on using small slip stitches with a matching thread. Remove the basting stitches.

9 Using matching thread, make small stitches along the seam of every other petal (as shown) to secure the Plate to the T-shirt.

The Dresden Plate design is fun and fresh, perfect for bright colors or floral prints. But experiment with your fabrics to try a different look.

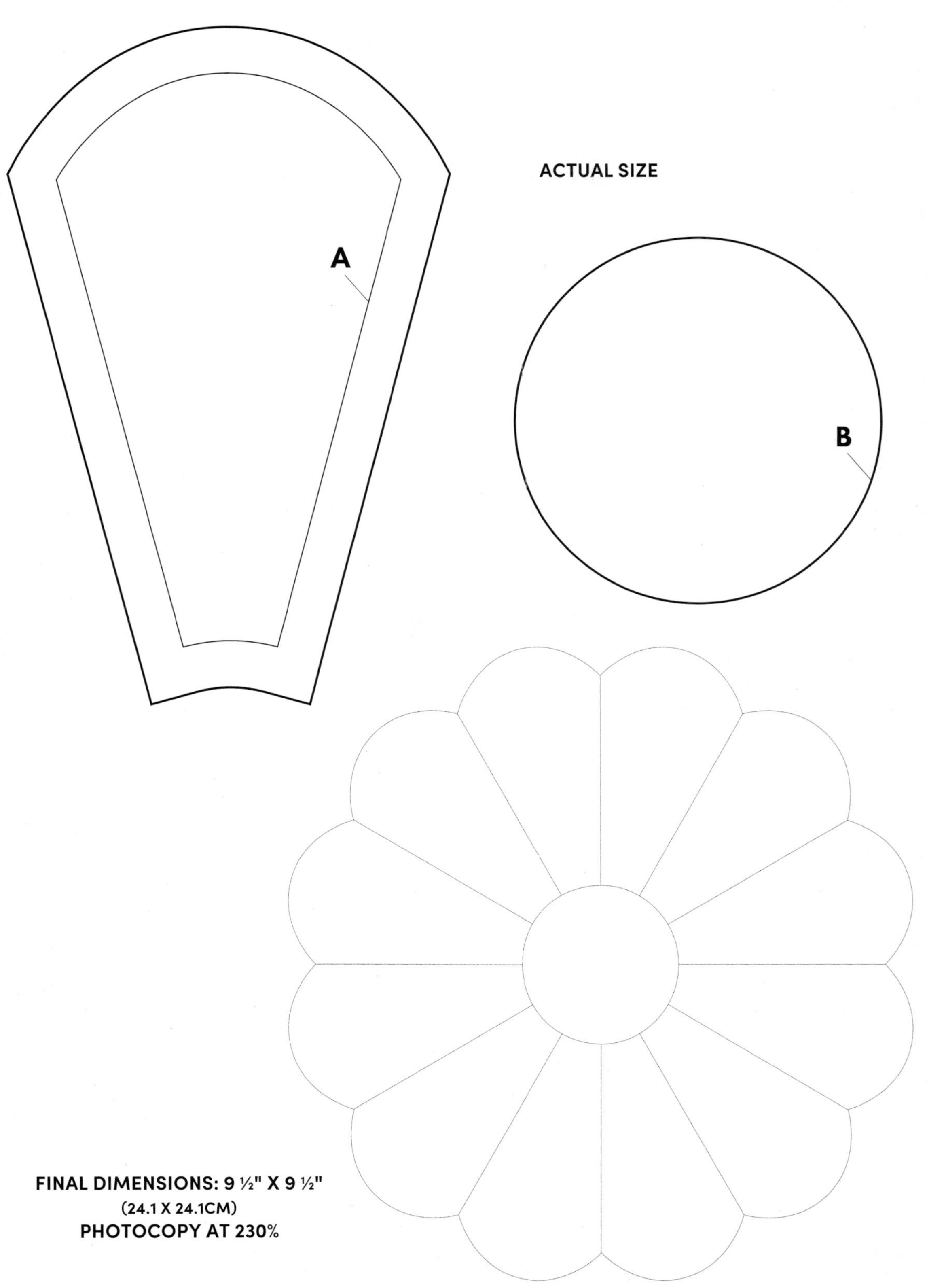
A
ACTUAL SIZE
B
FINAL DIMENSIONS: 9 ½" X 9 ½"
(24.1 X 24.1CM)
PHOTOCOPY AT 230%

T-Shirt with Rainbow Appliqué

Jazz up a plain T-shirt with this colorful appliqué design.

TECHNIQUES

- Traditional appliqué and iron-on appliqué
- *See pages 15 and 19.*

MATERIALS

- Double-sided iron-on interfacing
- Scraps of solid fabric
- 3¼" x 12½" (8.3 x 31.8cm) ecru fabric
- Transparent sewing thread
- T-shirt

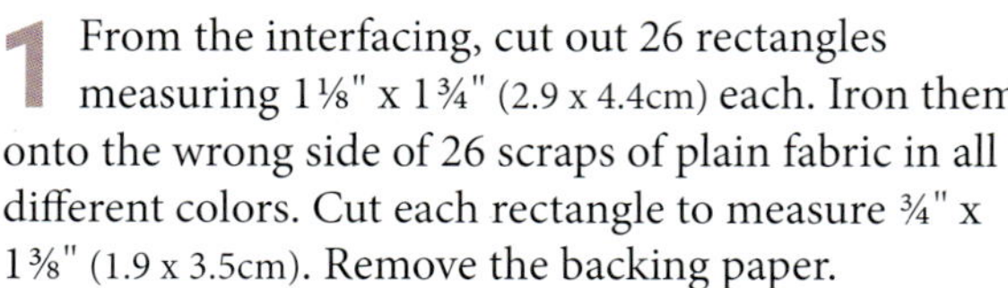

1 From the interfacing, cut out 26 rectangles measuring 1⅛" x 1¾" (2.9 x 4.4cm) each. Iron them onto the wrong side of 26 scraps of plain fabric in all different colors. Cut each rectangle to measure ¾" x 1⅜" (1.9 x 3.5cm). Remove the backing paper.

2 Turn a ⅜" (1cm) hem all the way around the ecru rectangle, then baste.

3 Place all the small rectangles on the right side of the ecru fabric in two rows, leaving about 1⁄16" (1.6mm) between them. Make sure the colors look good together.

4 On the bottom row, let the rectangles extend ⅜" (1cm) beyond the edge of the base fabric. Run your iron over all the rectangles, except for the fabric that extends beyond the bottom edge.

5 Machine stitch around the edges of each small rectangle and the ecru fabric. Remove the basting stitches.

6 Position the unit on the front of the T-shirt. Make small slip stitches all the way around it.

7 Remove the basting stitches.

Make sure you use consistent sizes and spacing to achieve this design.

Blouse with Embroidery and HSTs

This shirt has been personalized by adding half-square triangles (HSTs) to the cuffs, collar, and pocket. A few embroidered hearts have also been added.

TECHNIQUES

- Piecing, traditional appliqué, and embroidery
- *See pages 9, 15, and 20.*

MATERIALS

- Acetate sheet
- 9½" x 6" (24.1 x 16.5cm) ecru fabric
- Scraps of contrasting fabric
- Matching sewing threads
- Shirt with collar and cuffs
- Heat-erasable pen
- Embroidery threads

1 Trace Templates A and B (see page 33) onto a sheet of acetate. Cut out following the outlines.

2 For all the decorative elements, cut out the following shapes:

- 11 Triangle A in ecru fabric
- 11 Triangle A in contrasting fabrics
- 1 Triangle B in ecru fabric
- 1 Triangle B in a contrasting fabric

CUFFS

3 Join one ecru Triangle A and one contrasting Triangle A, sewing with right sides together and using the piecing technique. Press the seam allowances toward the darker triangle.

Make 4

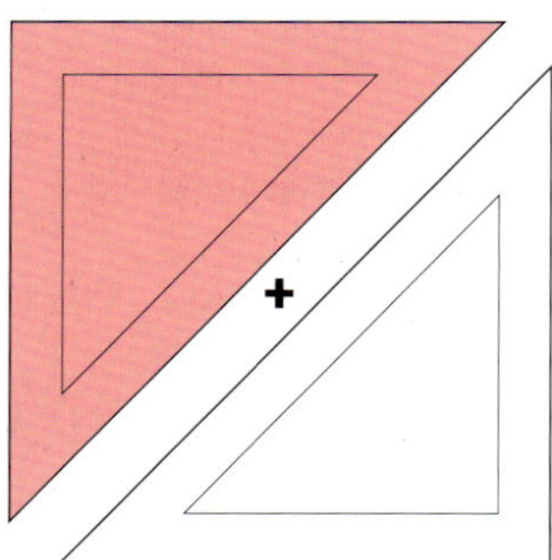

4 Cut off the seam allowance tails that are sticking out.

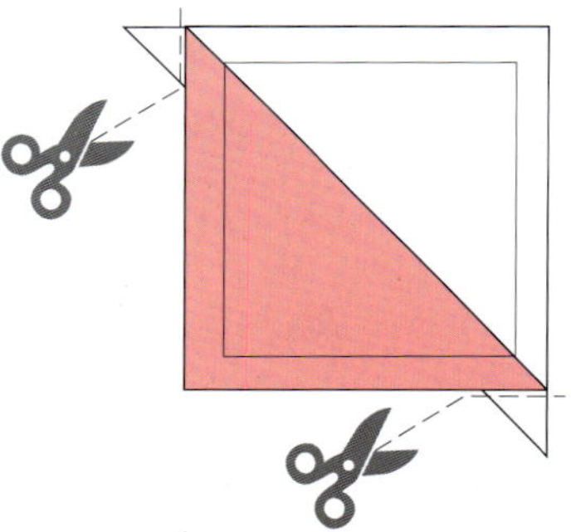

5 Repeat steps 3–4 three more times to make a total of four HSTs.

6 Join the four HSTs, stitching with right sides together, to form a strip. Make sure all the units are facing the same way.

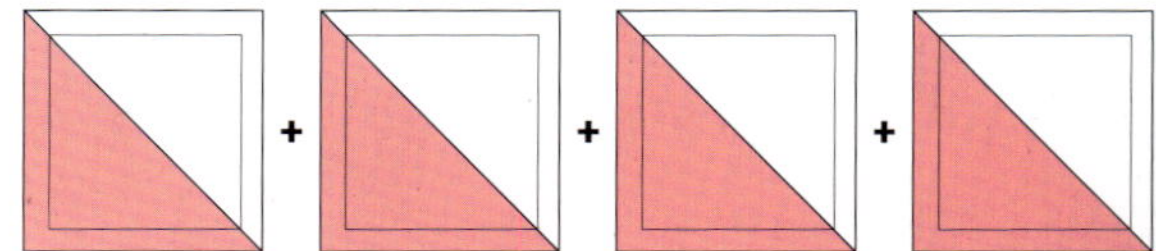

7 Turn a ¼" (6.4mm) hem all the way around, then baste. Position the strip on the cuff, baste, then sew on using small slip stitches. Remove the basting stitches.

8 Decorate the other cuff in the same way.

HEM AND COLLAR

9 Join one ecru Triangle A and one contrasting Triangle A, sewing with right sides together and using the piecing technique. Press the seam allowances toward the darker triangle. Cut off the tails of the seam allowances.

10 Repeat step 9 two times to make a total of three HSTs.

11 Turn a ¼" (6.4mm) hem all the way around, then baste.

12 Place one HST on the end of the collar. Place another square along the hem, one on each side. Sew on using small slip stitches. Remove the basting stitches.

SHIRT POCKET

13 Join the two B triangles (ecru and contrasting) in the same way as before.

14 Turn a ¼" (6.4mm) hem all the way around, then baste.

15 Position the HST on the pocket. Sew on using small slip stitches. Remove the basting stitches.

16 Embroider lines of running stitches following the shape of each triangle as shown.

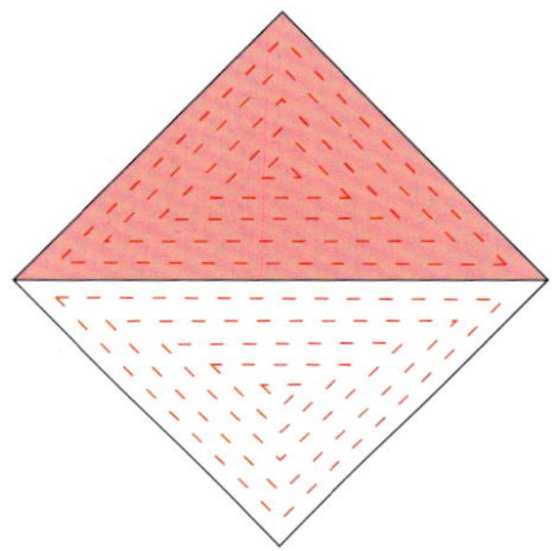

PLACKET

17 Using an erasable fabric pen, trace the hearts (see page 33) onto the placket. Embroider around the lines using small running stitches. Remove the marks.

These locations are just a suggestion; you may prefer a different look or need to cover different spots. Play with where you want to put your half-square triangles.

ACTUAL SIZE

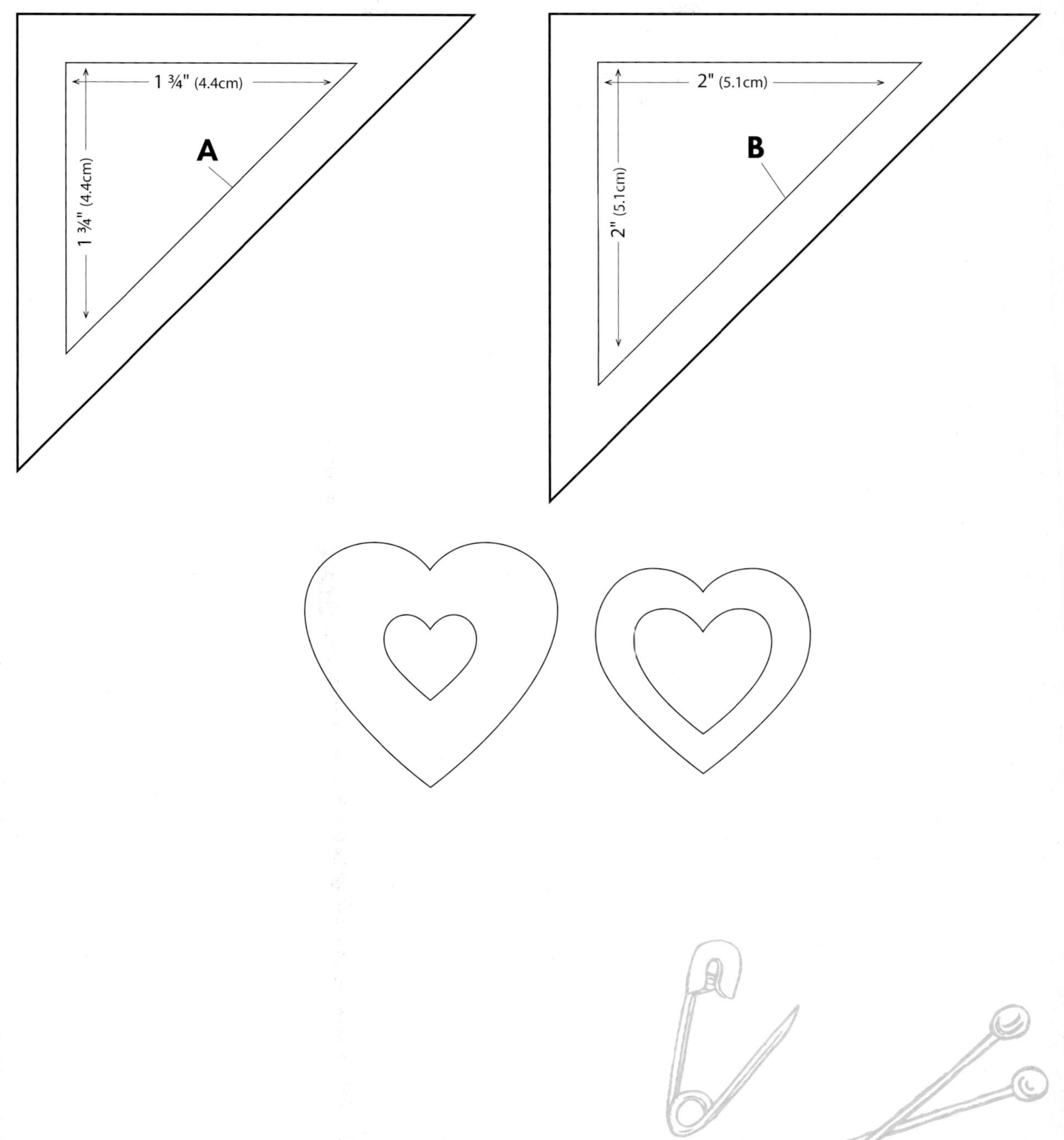

Star Block Blouse

By making quilt blocks and adding them to a beautiful shirt, you can create a truly original garment!

TECHNIQUES

- Piecing and traditional appliqué
- *See pages 9 and 15.*

MATERIALS

- Acetate sheet
- Scraps of white cotton fabric
- Scraps of light and medium blue cotton fabrics
- Matching threads
- Shirt with hidden placket

The templates include a ¼" (6.4mm) seam allowance. When piecing the triangles, remember to cut the tails of the seam allowances.

1 Transfer Templates A, B, C, and D (see page 37) onto a sheet of acetate, thin cardboard, or cardstock.

MAKING THE BLOCKS

The pattern is made up of four identical blocks.

2 To make one block, cut:

- 1 Triangle A and 2 Triangle B in medium blue fabric
- 2 Triangle C in light blue fabric
- 4 Triangle B and 2 Square D in white fabric

3 Join one blue Triangle B and one white Triangle B to form a half-square triangle (HST). Press the seam allowance toward the blue triangle.

4 Repeat to make a second HST.

Make 2

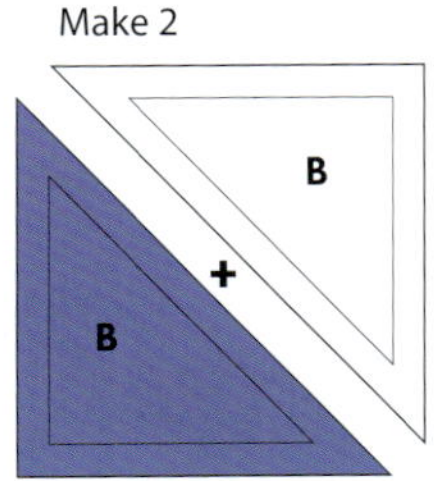

5 Join one white Square D to the side of one B/B HST. Repeat to make a second unit. Iron.

Make 2

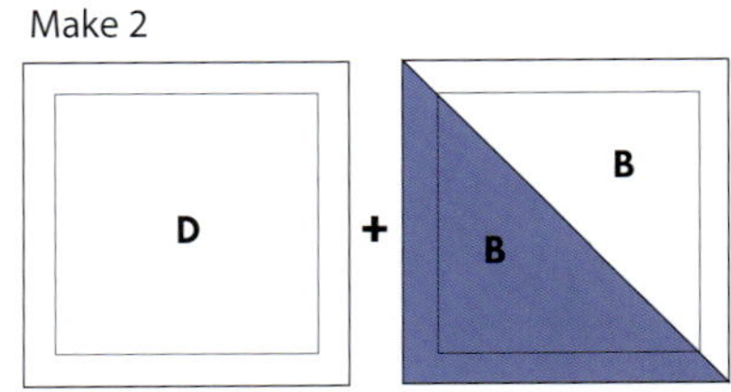

6 Join the two units, reversing the colors as shown.

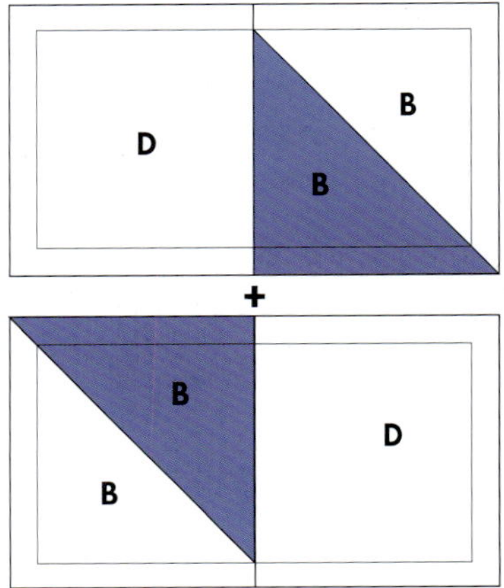

7 Join one white Triangle B to a short side of one blue Triangle C. Press the seam allowance toward the blue side.

8 Repeat step 7, but place the white triangle on the other short side (to make two mirrored units).

Make 2, mirrored

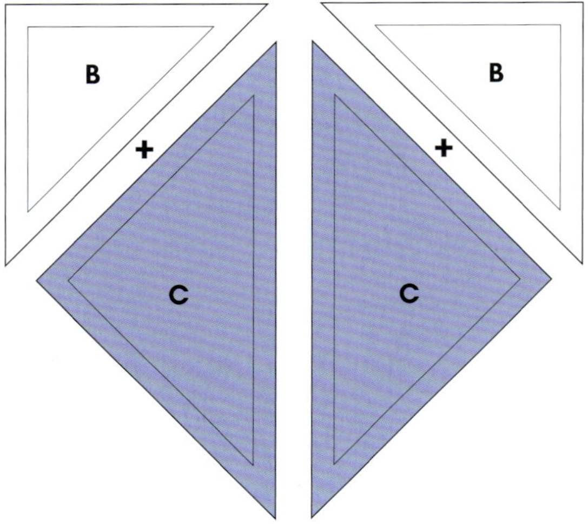

9 Join these two B/C units to the B/B/D square as shown.

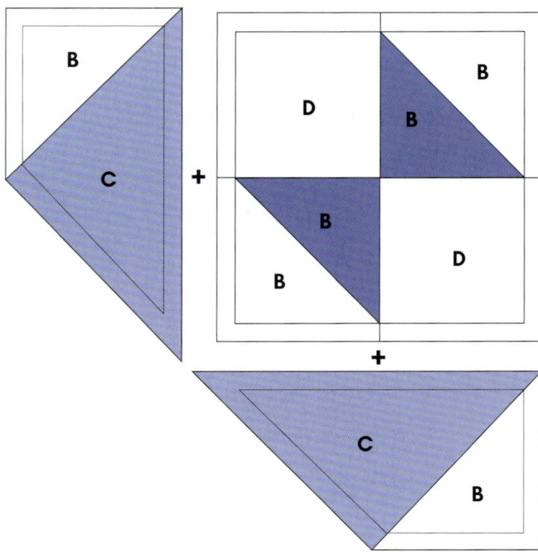

10 Add the blue Triangle A to complete the block. Iron.

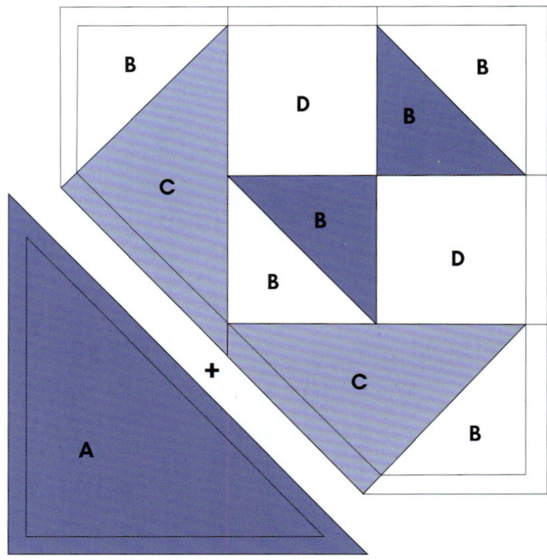

11 Repeat this process three more times to make a total of four blocks.

APPLIQUÉING

12 Cut a final 1½" x 1½" (3.8 x 3.8cm) square from the medium blue fabric. Turn a ¼" (6.4mm) hem all the way around, then baste.

13 In the same manner, turn a ¼" (6.4mm) hem all around the four blocks and baste.

14 Place the blocks on the shirt, on either side of the button placket. Leave a 1" (2.5cm) gap between the top and bottom row. Pin and baste.

15 Sew the blocks onto the shirt using small slip stitches in a matching thread.

16 Place the small blue square in the center, on the covered placket. Baste and sew on as before. Remove the basting stitches.

ACTUAL SIZE

C
Grainline
3 ⅛" (7.9cm)
D
1 ½" (3.8cm)
A
3 ⅛" (7.9cm)
Grainline
3 ⅛" (7.9cm)
B
Grainline
1 ½" (3.8cm)

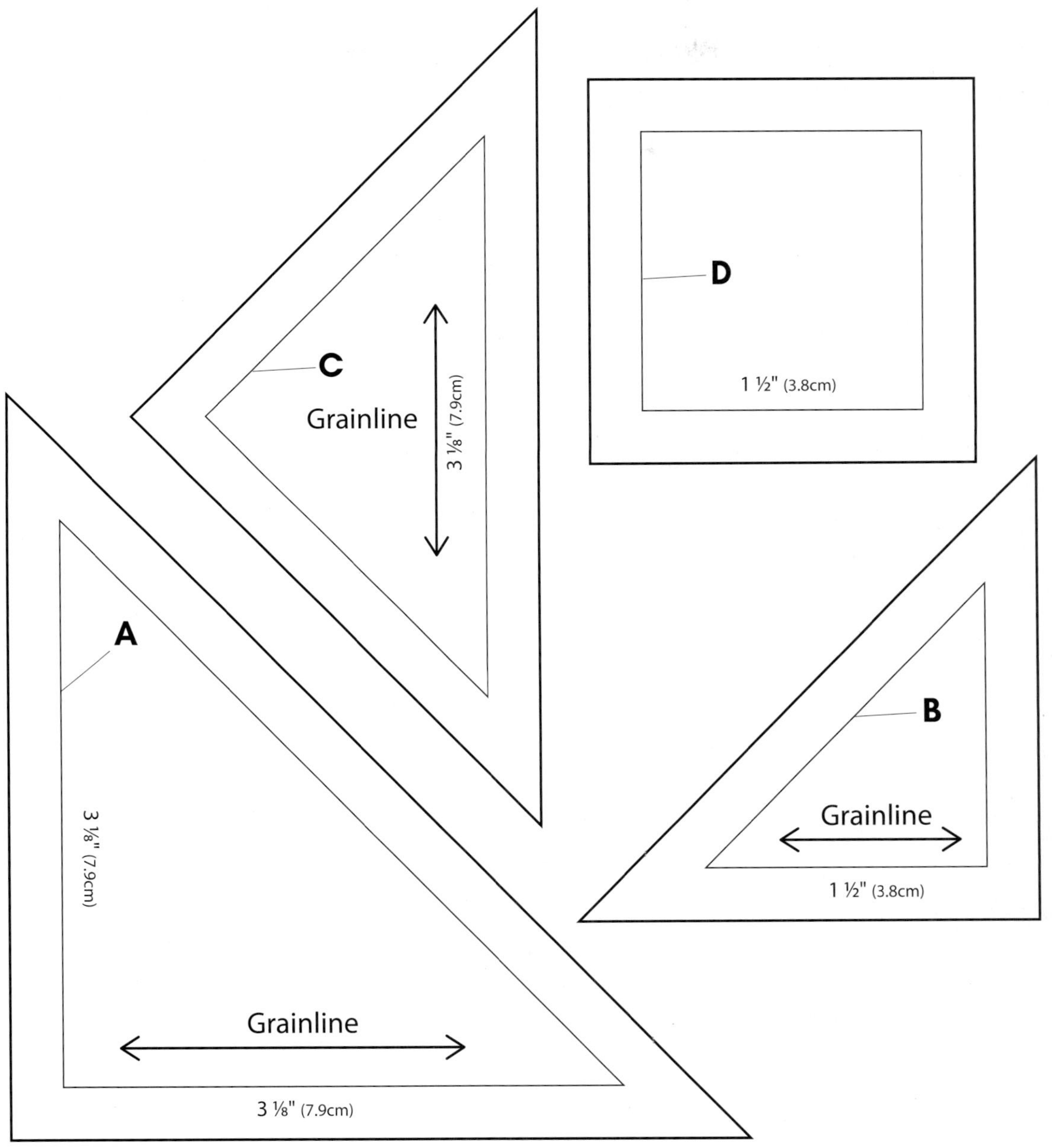

Shirt with Appliqué Detailing

Shades of blue and green brilliantly conceal stains on this light blue shirt.

TECHNIQUES

- Iron-on appliqué and embroidery
- *See pages 19 and 20.*

MATERIALS

- Double-sided iron-on interfacing
- Scraps of blue and green fabric
- Shirt with cuffs
- Matching sewing threads
- Heat-erasable pen
- Embroidery threads

SHIRT FRONT

1 Cut the interfacing into pieces measuring approximately 2½" x 3¼" (6.4 x 8.3cm).

2 Place the shiny side of the interfacing on the wrong side of a few fabric scraps. Iron and cut around the interfacing.

3 Cut about 15 small squares and rectangles between ¾" (1.9cm) and 2¾" (7cm) in size from the interfaced fabric pieces.

4 Remove the backing paper.

5 Arrange the shapes on either side of the shirt front. Press to fix them in place.

6 Secure the shapes with running stitches around the edges.

7 Using an erasable pen, draw lines on the shirt that connect the base fabric and the appliqué shapes. Embroider along the lines using the running stitch and varying the thread color. Erase the marks.

CUFF EDGING

8 From the blue and green fabric scraps, cut pieces measuring 2¼" x 2¼" (5.7 x 5.7cm). You'll need seven or eight pieces to make a strip, depending on your cuff's length.

9 Join the pieces, sewing with right sides together and a ¼" (6.4mm) sew allowance. Iron all the seam allowances in the same direction. Repeat to make an identical strip.

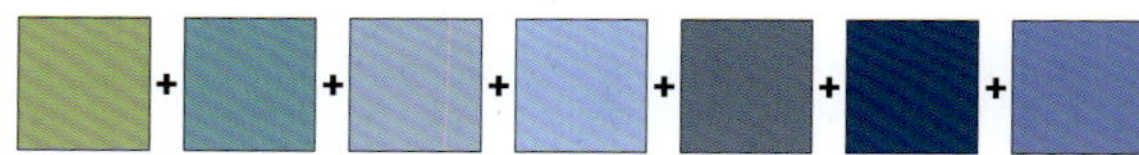

10 Fold one strip in half along its entire length, wrong sides together. Mark the center fold with an iron.

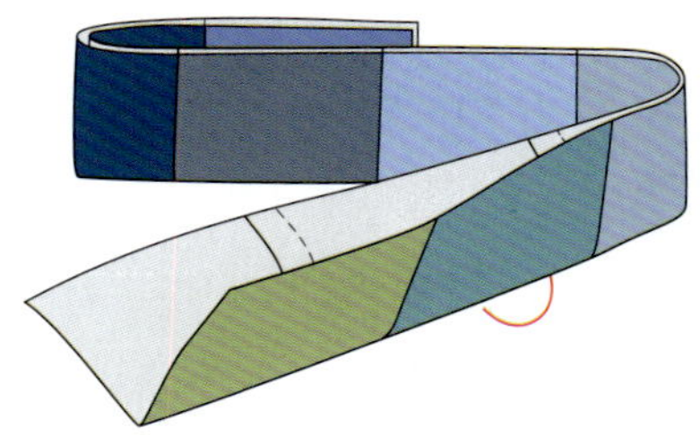

11 Place the strip on one cuff, right sides together, and fold both ends toward the inside. Once the strip has been folded over the edge, make sure the marked center line is directly above the end of the cuff. Machine stitch ⅜" (1cm) from the edge.

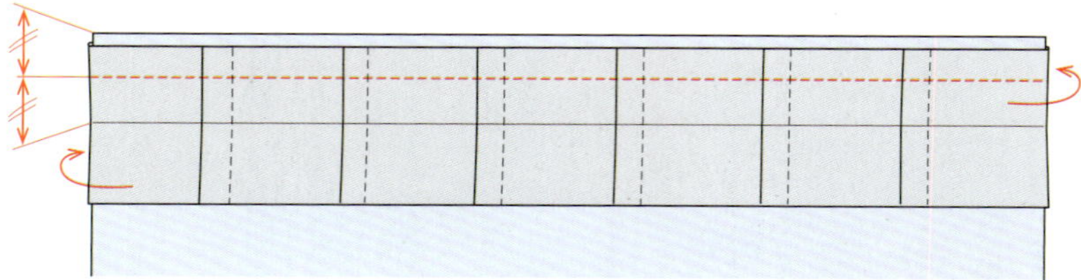

12 Fold the strip over the end of the cuff and turn a ⅜" (1cm) hem along the edge. Baste and secure with small blind stitches. Once sewn, the strip runs around the end of the cuff.

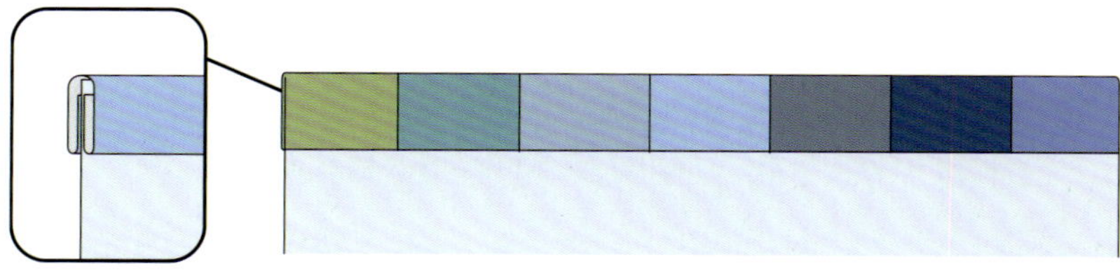

13 Do the same on the other cuff.

The embroidered stitches connect the shirt with the appliqué pieces, so don't be afraid to add a lot of lines. It's a subtle but important design element!

These cuff details are subtle, but they always get a ton of compliments. You'll want to add them onto all your clothes.

Shirt with Appliqué Circles

Circles cut out of striped fabric add pizzazz to this simple white shirt.

TECHNIQUE
- Traditional appliqué
- *See page 15.*

MATERIALS
- Acetate sheet
- 9½" x 9½" (24.1 x 24.1cm) blue-and-white stripe cotton fabric
- Matching thread
- White shirt

1 Trace Template A on the wrong side of the striped fabric. Cut out, adding an extra ¼" (6.4mm) seam allowance.

2 Turn a ¼" (6.4mm) hem all the way around and baste.

3 Place this circle on the bottom of one side of the shirt front, pin, then baste.

4 Slip stitch with matching thread, then remove the basting stitches.

5 Do the same with Template B. Place it over the placket at the top, wrapping it around to the inside so only a semicircle is showing on the outside.

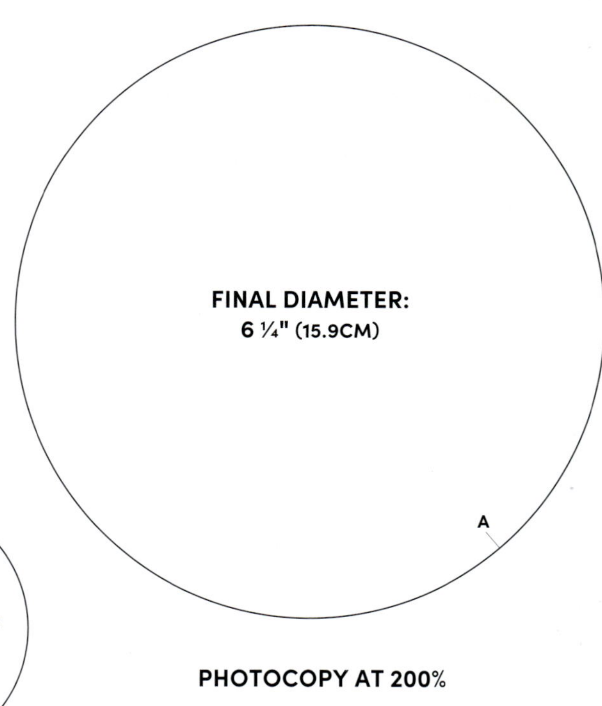

FINAL DIAMETER:
2 ¾" (7CM)
B

PHOTOCOPY AT 200%

Alphabet Shirt

A few letters cut out of scraps of colored fabric are scattered across a shirt, giving it a bespoke look.

TECHNIQUE
- Reverse appliqué
- *See page 18.*

MATERIALS
- Acetate sheet
- Shirt
- Scraps of solid fabric
- Matching threads

1 Trace a letter (see pages 46–47) onto the shirt and cut out inside the outline.

2 Place a scrap of fabric that is slightly larger than the cutout underneath and baste in place.

3 On the right side, use small backstitches to sew around the cutout letter, 1⁄16" (1.6mm) from the edge.

4 Cut the fabric underneath to 3⁄8" (1cm) from the stitching.

5 Remove the basting stitches.

6 Repeat the process with the other letters.

Here, I've used *M, A, R,* and *Z,* but you can choose any letters you like. This is the perfect way to customize clothing for friends and family.

M R
A Z

FINAL DIMENSIONS:
2" (5.1CM) HEIGHT FOR EACH LETTER
PHOTOCOPY AT 140%

Shirt with Appliqué Detailing

Beautiful floral fabrics add a dash of style to this modest shirt dress.

TECHNIQUES

- Iron-on appliqué and embroidery
- *See pages 19 and 20.*

MATERIALS

- Scraps of fabric with large floral prints
- Double-sided iron-on interfacing
- Long shirt or lightweight jacket
- Embroidery threads

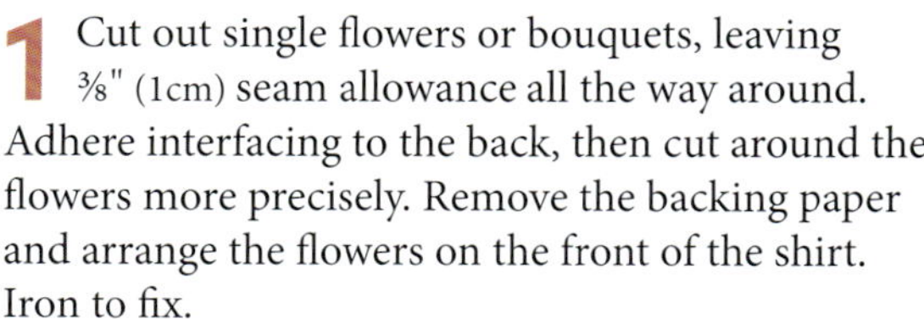

1 Cut out single flowers or bouquets, leaving ⅜" (1cm) seam allowance all the way around. Adhere interfacing to the back, then cut around the flowers more precisely. Remove the backing paper and arrange the flowers on the front of the shirt. Iron to fix.

2 Inside the flowers, sew in place using running stitches in various colors. Add a line or two of running stitches around each motif.

Be deliberate about your color choices so you know what the overall effect will be. Using a pink and teal thread helps emphasize the bright colors in the fabric, bringing a youthful look to the garment.

Sweater with Appliqué Flower

Petal shapes cut from colorful fabrics add life to this wool sweater.

TECHNIQUES

- Raw-edge appliqué and embroidery
- *See pages 17 and 20.*

MATERIALS

- Acetate sheet
- Scraps of wool fabric
- Embroidery threads
- Wool sweater

1 Using Template A, trace the shape onto 10 different pieces of fabric and cut them out. Using Templates B and C, trace and cut out two circles in any fabric you like.

2 Place Circle C on top of the Circle B and embroider two rows of running stitches around the center of the small circle.

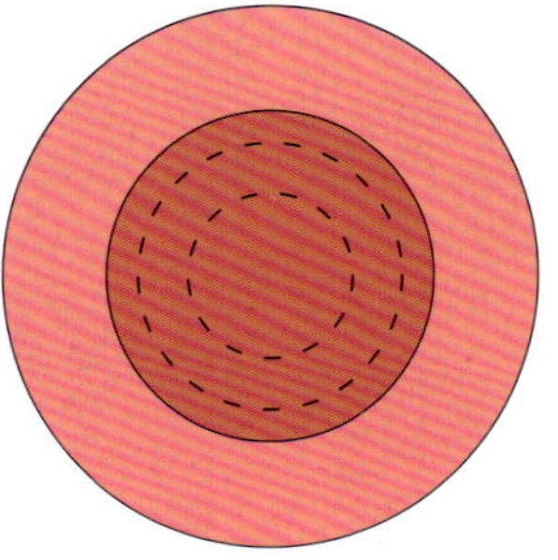

3 Arrange the A petals on the sweater and place the circles in the center, covering the ends of the petals. Pin and baste. Embroider the outline of the petals using a running stitch in matching threads. Embroider the edge of the large circle with a blanket stitch. Remove all the basting stitches.

FINAL HEIGHT:
5 ⅝" (14.3CM)

A

FINAL DIAMETER:
2 ¼" (5.7CM)

C

FINAL DIAMETER:
3 ½" (8.9CM)

B

PHOTOCOPY AT 155%

Sweater with Appliqué Denim Shapes

Scraps of denim cut into geometric shapes cleverly conceal holes in an old sweater.

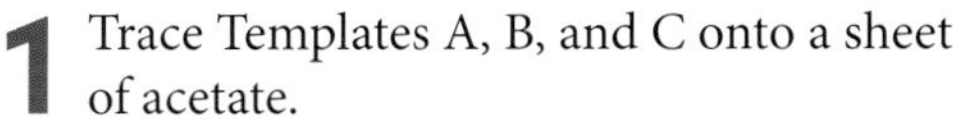

TECHNIQUES

- Traditional appliqué and embroidery
- *See pages 15 and 20.*

MATERIALS

- Acetate sheet
- Scraps of denim
- Matching sewing threads
- Sweater
- Embroidery threads
- Off-white wool yarn
- Tapestry needle

1 Trace Templates A, B, and C onto a sheet of acetate.

2 On the wrong side of the scraps of denim, trace Templates B and C once and Template A twice. Cut out, adding ¼" (6.4mm) all the way around.

3 Following the traditional appliqué instructions (page 15), attach the shapes to the front of the sweater.

4 Embroider a running stitch around the appliqué motifs.

5 Using the yarn and tapestry needle, make large stitches around the neckline and before the bottom of the sleeves.

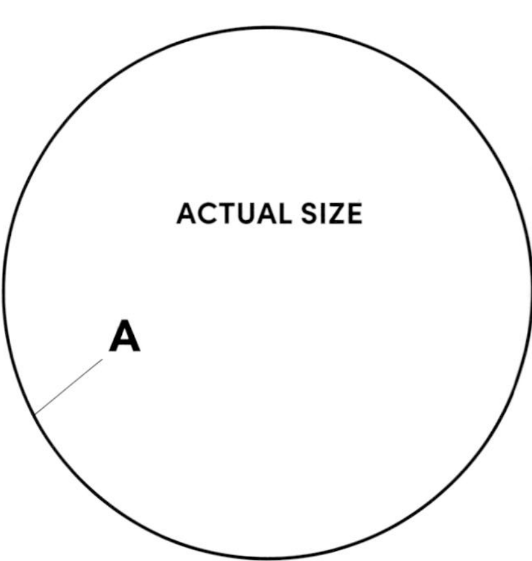

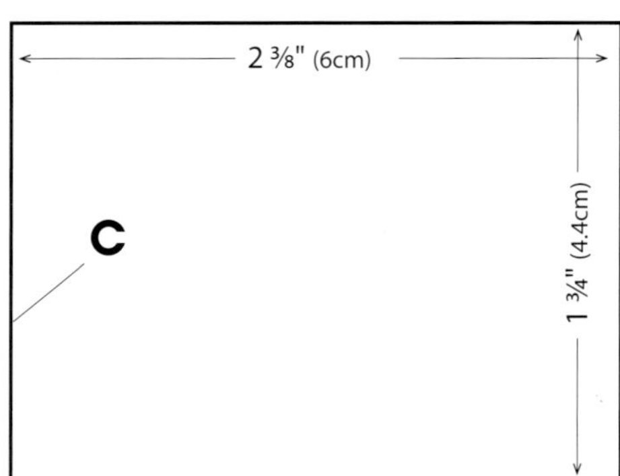

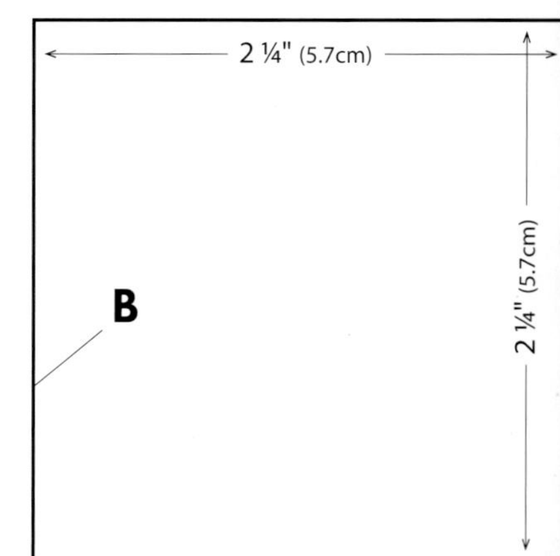

Sweater with Crazy Quilt Elbow Patches

Scraps of colorful fabric give new life to this sweater that's worn through at the elbows

TECHNIQUE

- Crazy quilt
- *See page 12.*

MATERIALS

- Double-sided iron-on interfacing
- Scraps of cotton fabric
- Wool sweater
- Embroidery threads

1 Trace the elbow pad template twice onto the backing paper of the double-sided iron-on interfacing. Make the two elbow pads using the crazy quilt technique (page 12).

2 Embroider each piece of fabric with a running stitch, angling each section in a different direction.

3 Place the elbow pads on the sleeves and baste. Sew around the edges in blanket stitch, then remove the basting stitches.

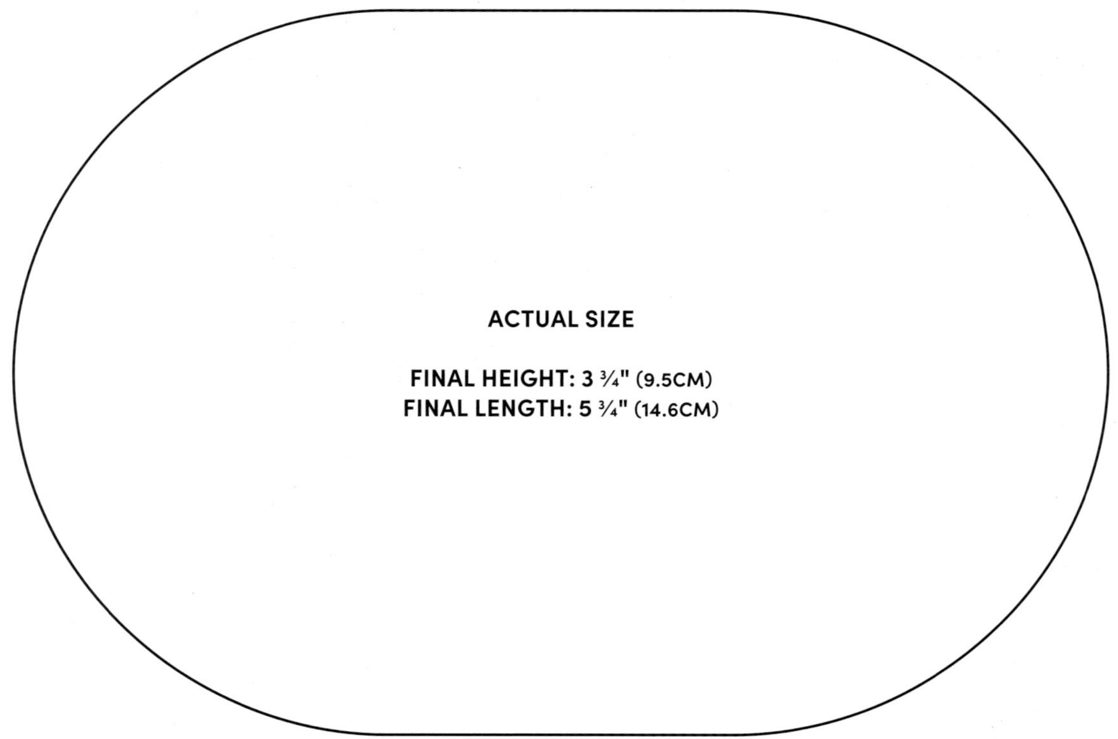

Women's Sweater-Vest

This sleeveless sweater makes use of pieces salvaged from old, damaged sweaters.

Tip: It's best to put this sweater together using an overlocker with a 3- or 4-thread overlock stitch. But you can also use your domestic machine with a zigzag or stretch stitch. This will prevent the stitching from breaking and ensure that your stretch fabric retains all of its properties.

TECHNIQUES
- Piecing and embroidery
- *See pages 9 and 20.*

MATERIALS
- 6 pieces from old sweaters in blue, green, and gray
- Matching sewing threads
- Jersey needle
- 1 piece from a sweater in black, approx. 24" x 28" (61 x 71.1cm)
- Tailor's chalk
- 1 piece of thin sweater fabric in brown
- Embroidery thread (optional)

PATCHWORK FRONT

Cut the following pieces from the blue, green, and gray sweater fabrics:

- 1 Rectangle A, 7½" x 10" (19.1 x 25.4cm)
- 1 Rectangle B, 9½" x 12¼" (24.1 x 31.1cm)
- 1 Rectangle C, 9" x 10" (22.9 x 25.4cm)
- 1 Rectangle D, 9" x 12¼" (24.1 x 31.1cm)
- 1 Rectangle E, 10" x 13" (25.4 x 33cm)
- 1 Rectangle F, 4½" x 12¼" (11.4 x 31.1cm)
- 1 Rectangle G, 7½" x 12¼" (19.1 x 31.1cm)

1 Join Rectangles A, C, and E, sewing with right sides together, to form the Left Side.

2 Join Rectangles B, D, F, and G, sewing with right sides together, to form the Right Side.

3 Finish by joining the Right and Left Sides, sewing with right sides together.

4 After sewing each seam, overcast the seam allowances and press them to one side with an iron.

ASSEMBLING THE BODY

5 Position and center the Front Template (see page 59) on the Patchwork Front. Pin and outline with chalk, then cut around the line.

6 Position the Back Template (see page 59) on the black sweater fabric. Pin and outline with chalk, then cut around the line.

7 Place the Patchwork Front onto the Back with the right sides together. Pin the sides and shoulders, then baste. Machine stitch and overcast the seam allowances, if necessary.

NECKLINE

8 From the brown sweater fabric, cut a strip measuring 1½" x 29½" (3.8 x 74.9cm).

9 Place the strip around the neckline, right sides together, starting at the center back.

10 Cut the end at a 45-degree angle and fold under ⅜" (1cm).

11 Start sewing ¾" (1.9cm) from the beginning of the strip and ¼" (6.4mm) from the edge.

12 When you get back to the starting point, make sure that the strip extends slightly beyond the section that has already been sewn. Cut the end at a 45-degree angle, overlap it, then finish sewing.

13 Fold the strip over to the reverse side using your finger, then iron. Stitch in place with slip stitches and matching thread.

HEM

14 Cut a strip measuring 1½" x 45" (3.8 x 114.3cm) from the brown sweater fabric (or two strips measuring 1½" x 22½" [3.8 x 57.2cm], then join for the required length).

15 Repeat the steps for the neckline, but without pulling the strip, as it is the same length as the bottom of the sweater-vest.

ARMHOLES

Option 1:

16 Overcast the edge of the armholes and fold ⅜" (1cm) toward the wrong side. Baste, then sew with slip stitches.

17 Embroider a blanket stitch ¼" (6.4mm) from the edge.

Option 2:

18 Finish the same as the neckline by cutting two strips of brown sweater fabric, each measuring 1½" x 14½" (3.8 x 36.8cm).

Try adding other appliqué elements from the rest of the book to further customize this sweater-vest.

Test Square:
2" x 2" (5.1 x 5.1cm)

Star Sweater

A simple motif added to a sweater with a hole instantly revamps it, as if by magic.

TECHNIQUES

- Reverse appliqué and embroidery
- *See pages 18 and 20.*

MATERIALS

- Heat-erasable pen or tailor's chalk
- Sweater
- Scraps of wool fabric
- Embroidery threads

1 Using an erasable pen or chalk, trace the Template A onto the front of the sweater, making sure it's in the center. Carefully cut out the inside. Insert a larger piece of wool fabric underneath the cutout, pin it in place, then baste. Sew small blanket stitches around the outline of the star to secure the two pieces together. Cut the fabric underneath to ⅜" (1cm) from the stitching, then remove the basting stitches.

2 As before, trace Template B in the center of A. Repeat the reverse appliqué technique.

Mix up the embroidery stitches and thread colors for added interest on your design.

3 Embroider lines of running stitches around the inside of both shapes, then embroider a star stitch in the center.

A

B

FINAL DIMENSIONS:
8" X 7 ½" (20.3 X 19.1CM)

PHOTOCOPY AT 220%

Geometric Appliqué Hoodie

Bits of fabric scattered across this hoodie in a tone-on-tone motif artfully conceal stains.

TECHNIQUE
- Traditional appliqué
- *See page 15.*

MATERIALS
- Scraps of solid fabric in shades of the same color
- Matching threads
- Hoodie

1 Cut pieces **A**, **B**, **C**, and **D** out of four different fabrics, following the measurements below (which include ¼" [6.4mm] seam allowances all around):

- 1 Rectangle A, 5¼" x 4¾" (13.3 x 12.1cm)
- 1 Rectangle B, 3" x 2¼" (7.6 x 5.7cm)
- 1 Rectangle C, 3⅛" x 7¼" (7.9 x 18.4cm)
- 1 Rectangle D, 2½" x 3⅛" (6.4 x 7.9cm)

2 Turn a ¼" (6.4mm) hem all the way around each rectangle (except for one long side on **A**, as this will be slipped under **C**), then baste.

3 On the front of the hoodie, place the rectangles in this order: **A**, **B**, **C**, **D**. Rectangle **B** should overlap halfway across A. Rectangle **C** should overlap **A** by ¼" (6.4mm). Rectangle **D** overlaps both **A** and **C**.

4 Pin as you go, then baste. Stitch each piece using small slip stitches.

5 Remove the basting stitches.

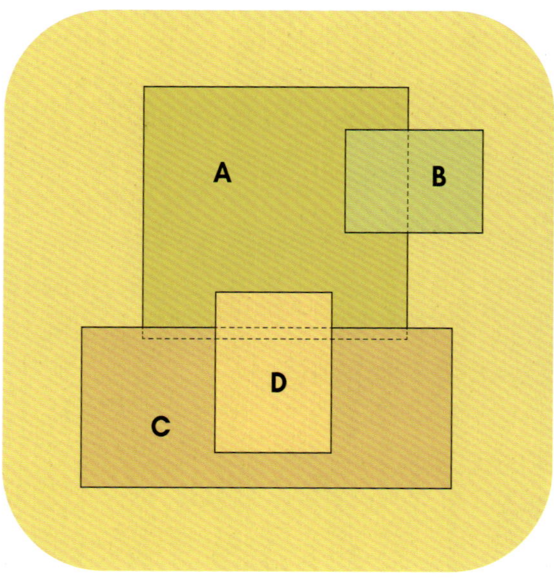

Placing these geometric shapes at a slight angle softens the design.

Leaf Dress

Appliqué leaves around the neckline and contrasting fabric on the sleeves and hem revitalize a dress that's frayed at the edges.

TECHNIQUES

- Iron-on appliqué, raw-edge appliqué, and embroidery
- *See pages 19, 17, and 20.*

MATERIALS

- Acetate sheet
- Scraps of sturdy fabric, such as wool, in dark colors
- Double-sided iron-on interfacing
- Matching sewing threads
- Scraps of thin fabric, such as linen
- Embroidery threads
- Dress
- Scraps of fabric in a contrasting color to the dress

NECKLINE

1 Trace the outline of Templates A1 and B1 (see page 66) onto the sheet of acetate. Cut them out.

2 In the wool fabric, cut out five Template A1 pieces and six Template B1pieces. Do not add seam allowances.

3 Follow the iron-on appliqué technique (page 19) for A1 and B1.

4 On the interfacing backing paper, trace Template A2 five times and Template B2 six times. Cut out all pieces, allowing an extra ¼" (6.4mm) all the way around.

5 Iron the A2 and B2 pieces onto the back of the linen fabric. Cut them out following the lines. Remove the backing paper from the A2 leaves and iron them onto the A1 leaves. Using different colors, embroider around and inside the leaves using the following stitches: running stitch, straight stitch, cross-stitch, star stitch, and French knot.

6 Appliqué the B2 leaves onto the B1 leaves in the same way.

7 Arrange all the leaves around the neckline, alternating the sizes. Baste, then sew onto the dress using small running stitches in a matching thread. Remove the basting stitches.

SLEEVES

When adding a contrasting border to the bottom of sleeves, the end must be plain, have no extra detailing, and have a standard hem.

8 Measure around the bottom of the sleeves.

9 Cut two strips measuring 3⅛" (7.9cm) x (sleeve circumference + ¾" [1.9cm]).

10 Place the two short sides of the strip with the right sides together, and sew ¼" (6.4mm) from the edge. Iron the seam allowances open. Your strip now forms a ring.

11 Fold the strip in half, wrong sides together, along its entire length. Press to mark the center.

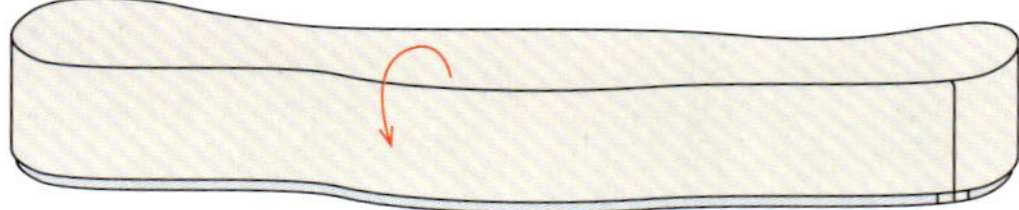

12 Unfold the strip and pin to the bottom of a sleeve, with right sides together. Align the seams and make sure that, once the strip has been folded over the edge, the center crease is directly above the bottom edge of the sleeve. Stitch ⅜" (1cm) from the edge of the strip.

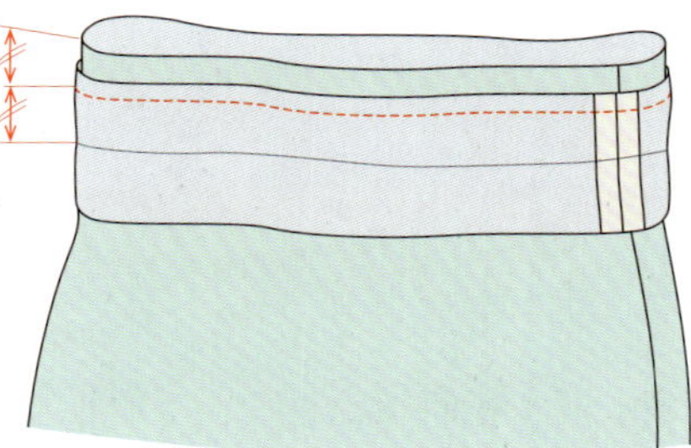

13 Fold the strip over to the inside. The center crease will run around the bottom of the sleeve. Fold the edge under ¼" (6.4mm) and pin in place. Baste, then sew with blind stitches.

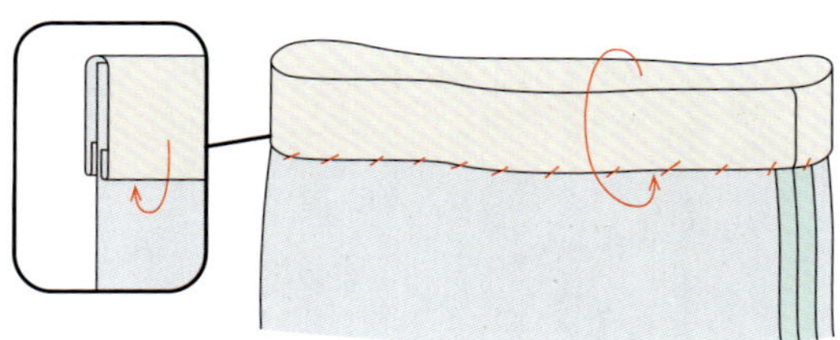

HEM

14 Repeat the steps for the sleeves, cutting a strip that is 3⅛" (7.9cm) x (total hem circumference + ¾" [1.9cm]).

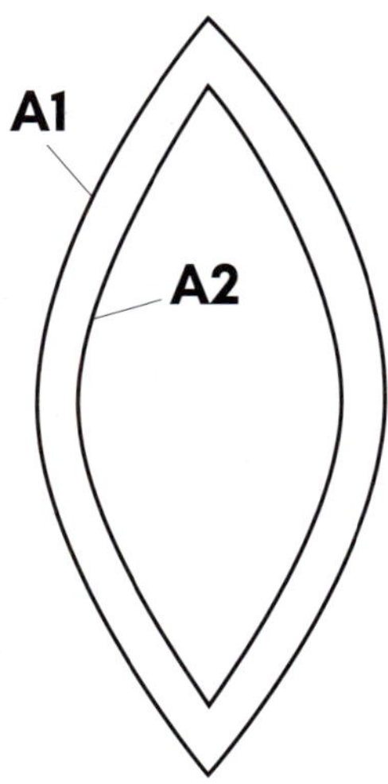

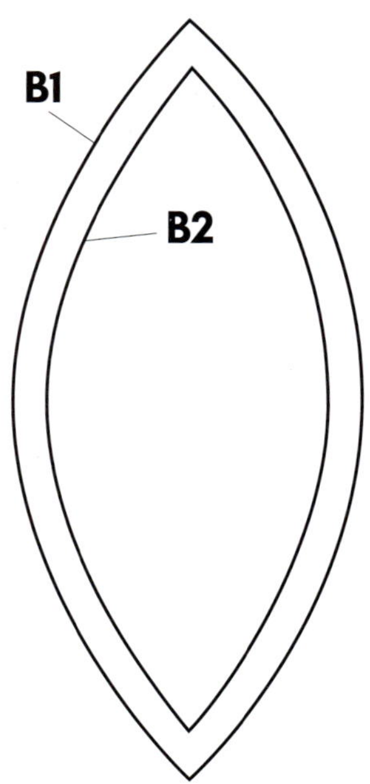

Here's your chance to play around with embroidery stitches! Don't be too worried about making them perfect; the raw edge of the appliqué already lends a relaxed style to this project, so you can have fun.

Patchwork Jeans

A few patches cut from old pairs of jeans are all you need to give these worn-out pants a new lease on life.

TECHNIQUES

- Piecing and traditional appliqué
- *See pages 9 and 15.*

MATERIALS

- Scraps of denim fabric in different shades
- Jeans
- Matching threads

RIGHT LEG

1 Cut six pieces from the denim scraps, using the dimensions in the diagram (right) as a guide. Remember to add ¼" (6.4mm) all around.

2 Turn a ¼" (6.4mm) hem all the way around and baste.

3 Arrange the pieces on the right leg (as worn), laying them edge to edge.

4 To sew by machine, you will need to take out the outer leg seam with a seam ripper first. Apply the patches, then re-sew and overcast that seam.

LEFT LEG

5 Cut six squares measuring 2" x 2" (5.1 x 5.1cm). Join them together in a strip, one after the other, sewing with the right sides together and with ¼" (6.4mm) seam allowance. Press the seam allowances open.

6 Measure the width of your pants where you want to position the band.

7 If necessary, trim your band to match the width of your pants + ¾" (1.9cm).

8 Turn a ¼" (6.4mm) hem all the way around and baste.

9 Cut a second strip, measuring 2⅜" (6cm) x (the width of your pants + ¾" [1.9cm]).

10 Turn a ¼" (6.4mm) hem all the way around and baste.

11 Place the two strips, one above the other, on the left leg. Sew them on either by hand using small slip stitches or by machine.

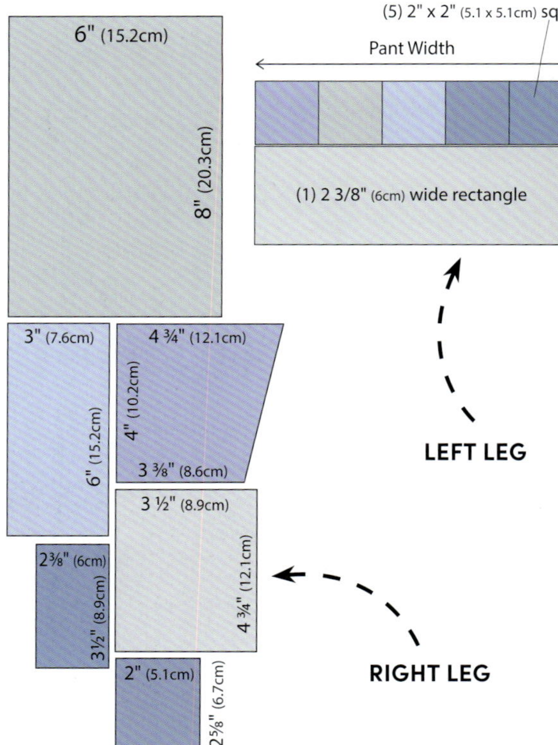

PHOTOCOPY AT 500%

Patchwork Scarf

A simple and effective way to give new life to old T-shirts.

TECHNIQUE

- Piecing
- *See page 9.*

MATERIALS

- 10 pieces of jersey fabric, from old T-shirts, in different colors
- Matching threads
- Jersey needle

1 From the T-shirts, cut squares and rectangles that are 7" (17.8cm) wide and of varying lengths: 3" (7.6cm), 4" (10.2cm), 5" (12.7cm), 6" (15.2cm), 7½" (19.1cm), 10" (25.4cm), etc.

2 Allowing a seam allowance of ¼" (6.4mm), join the pieces with the right sides together, alternating colors until you have a strip that is about 65" (165.1cm) long.

3 In the same manner, make a second strip. It does not need to be identical.

Tip: Although it's best to sew stretchy fabrics like jersey using a stretch stitch on your sewing machine, this item doesn't need to retain its stretch. You can therefore sew using a straight stitch when joining the different pieces together to make up the patchwork strip.

4 Place the two strips together, with right sides together, and sew along the two long sides, ¼" (6.4mm) from the edges.

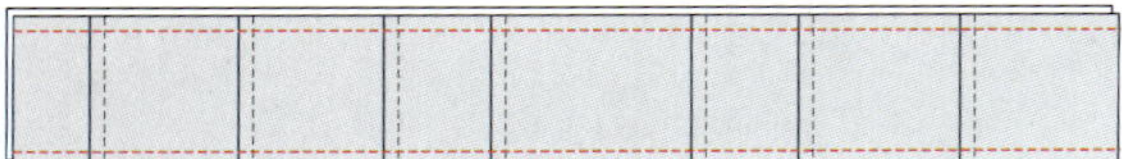

5 Turn the scarf right side out and press with an iron.

6 At both ends, turn a ¼" (6.4mm) double-fold hem. Pin and baste. Sew by hand using small slip stitches, then remove the basting stitches.

If you use a T-shirt with a logo, use a pressing cloth to iron that area of the fabric. The logo can melt under direct heat.

Pants with Crazy Quilt Cuffs

These pants have been given a fresh new look by adding strips of crazy quilt to the hems, waistband, and pocket edges.

TECHNIQUE
- Crazy quilt
- *See page 12.*

MATERIALS
- Iron-on interfacing
- Scraps of wool fabric
- Embroidery threads
- Cropped (7/8 length) pants
- Matching sewing threads

TROUSER CUFFS

In contrast to the traditional crazy quilt method, the double-sided iron-on interfacing is replaced here by a one-sided iron-on interfacing.

1 Measure around the hem of your pants.

2 Cut two interfacing strips measuring approximately 3¼" (8.3cm) x (hem circumference + ¾" [1.9cm]).

3 Place one interfacing strip with the glue side facing up, and arrange small pieces of fabric of different colors and shapes on top. They should overlap slightly. Make sure they extend beyond the interfacing. Once done, press with a hot iron to hold the pieces of fabric in place.

4 If you have left gaps in any part to show the interfacing, place a damp cloth or piece of fabric over the strip before pressing to prevent the adhesive from sticking to the iron.

5 Trim off the excess fabric extending beyond the interfacing.

6 Embroider each shape with running stitches.

7 Place the two short sides of the strip with the right sides together, and sew ¼" (6.4mm) from the edge. Iron the seam allowances open. Your strip now forms a ring.

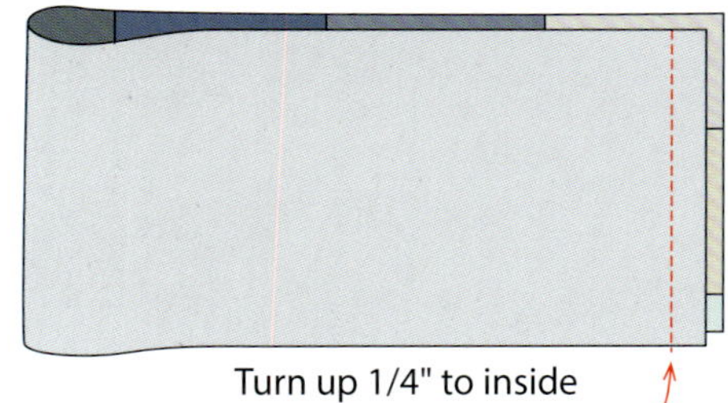

8 At the bottom of the strip, turn ¼" (6.4mm) toward the wrong side to form the hem. Baste and sew.

9 Slide the edge of the strip that does not have a hem inside one of the pant legs, from the

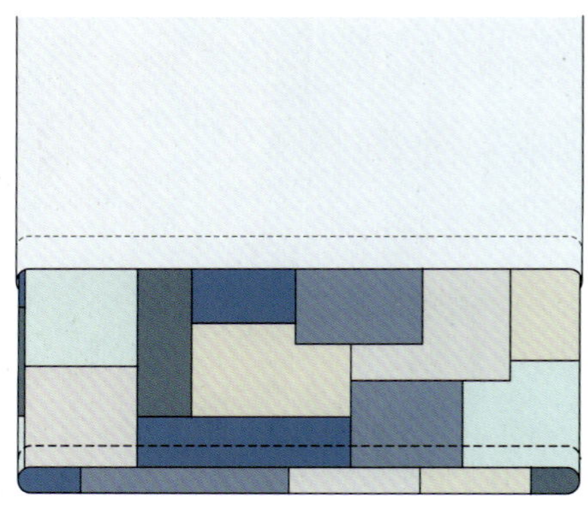

bottom, and overlap them by ⅜" (1cm). Machine stitch to secure the two elements together.

10 Make the other cuff for the second leg in the same way.

WAISTBAND

11 Measure the height of your waistband.

12 From the various fabric scraps, cut rectangles of varying lengths between 2" (5.1cm) and 3½" (8.9cm) and that are the height of your waistband + ¾" (1.9cm).

13 Join the pieces, sewing with right sides together and ¼" (6.4mm) seam allowance, until you have a strip that is the length you want.

14 Turn a ¼" (6.4mm) hem all the way around. Position the strip on the waistband and baste, then sew it in place using small slip stitches all the way around, making sure that the strip lies perfectly flat against the waistband.

15 Remove the basting stitches.

POCKET HEM

16 From your chosen fabric, cut two strips measuring 1½" (3.8cm) wide x (the width of your pockets + ¾" [1.9cm]).

17 Take one of the strips and fold it in half lengthwise, with the wrong sides together,

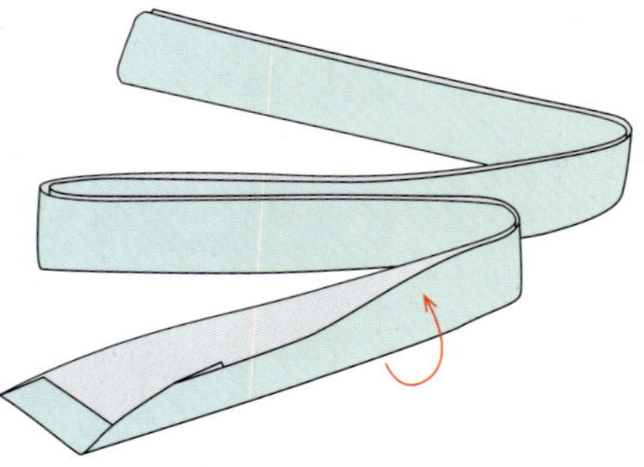

and press the fold with an iron.

18 Open the strip and turn a ⅜" (1cm) hem at both ends.

19 Pin the strip along the opening of one pocket, with the right sides together and the edges aligned. Sew ⅜" (1cm) from the edge of the

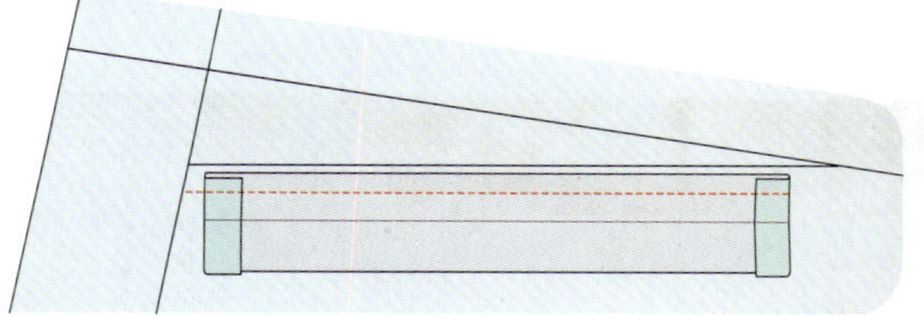

strip by hand or machine (depending on which is easier).

20 Fold the strip inside the pocket. The crease should run along the edge of the pocket opening. Turn ¼" (6.4mm) along the free edge and pin in place. Baste, then sew with blind stitches.

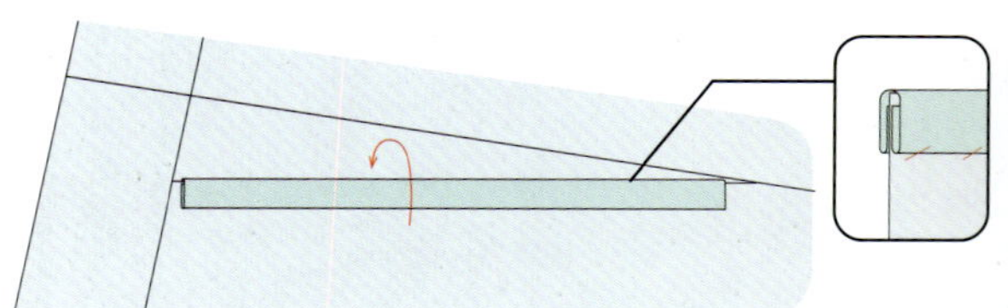

21 Repeat for the other pocket.

You might want to use full-length pants for this project instead of cropped pants. For example, taller folks might have new pants that aren't long enough, or shorter folks might have frayed hems that can be cut and hidden.

Denim Shorts with Lace

A pair of ripped jeans is reinvented as boho shorts by adding a touch of lace.

TECHNIQUE
- Iron-on appliqué
- *See page 19.*

MATERIALS
- Old jeans or denim shorts
- Lace trim
- Matching thread

SHORTS HEM

1 Cut the jeans to the length you want for your shorts. Here, the legs measure 12½" (31.8cm) from the waistband.

2 Measure the hem circumference of your shorts.

3 Cut two strips of lace to the desired width x (the hem circumference + ¾" [1.9cm]).

4 Place the two short sides of one strip with the right sides together, and sew ¼" (6.4mm) from the edge. Iron the seam allowances open. Your strip now forms a ring.

5 Slide the lace inside one leg of the shorts, from the bottom, and overlap them by ⅜" (1cm). Baste, then machine stitch to secure the two elements together.

6 Do the same on the other leg.

BELT

7 Cut a strip of lace wide enough and long enough to make a belt.

8 The one here measures 59" (149.9cm) for size 4 jeans.

APPLIQUÉ

9 Place a lace appliqué motif on one of the legs of the shorts and sew around the edge using small slip stitches.

Don't worry about disguising the frayed hem, as it adds to the boho chic look. But you can always fold the hem if desired.

RICOH
500 GX
Glossier.
balm
dotcom

Tailored Vest with Appliqué Detailing

Appliqué and embroidered striped fabric pieces brighten up this ultra-classy tailored vest.

TECHNIQUES
- Raw-edge appliqué and embroidery
- *See pages 17 and 20.*

MATERIALS
- Scraps of striped fabric
- Tailored vest
- Embroidery threads

1 Cut rectangles of different sizes from the striped fabrics.

2 Here, the smallest pieces are 1" x 1½" (2.5 x 3.8cm) and the largest are 2⅜" x 4" (6 x 10.2cm).

3 Without turning a hem, position the rectangles on the two front edges of the vest (using the photos as a guide), and slightly overlap some of the pieces. At the neckline, fold over the rectangles that extend beyond the edge.

4 Once you're happy with your design, pin in place and baste.

5 Using different colors, embroider large running stitches across all the pieces, varying the direction of the stitches (horizontal or vertical). Remove the basting stitches.

Notice how I alternated thread colors in each row or column of running stitches. This adds another interesting element that boosts the design of the striped fabric.

Tweed Jacket with Patches

This jacket has had a makeover: the lapels have been covered with a different fabric, a new trim has been added to the ends of the sleeves, two elbow patches have been sewn on, and small pieces of fabric have been appliquéd on. It's as good as new!

TECHNIQUE

- Raw-edge appliqué
- *See page 17.*

MATERIALS

- Acetate sheet
- Scraps of wool fabric
- Tweed jacket with lapels and buttoned cuffs
- Matching sewing threads
- Embroidery threads

LAPELS

1 Trace the shape of the lapel onto a sheet of acetate. Add ⅜" (1cm) all around and cut out the template.

2 Trace and cut out the piece twice, as mirror images, from wool fabric.

3 Place a piece on the corresponding original lapel, right side up. Pin in place, turning a ⅜" (1cm) hem all the way around to align the edges. Sew on using small slip stitches in a matching thread.

4 Cover the other lapel in the same way.

SLEEVE ENDS

5 Measure around the bottom of the sleeves, from slit edge to slit edge.

6 In a wool fabric, cut two strips measuring 2½" (6.4cm) x (the sleeve hem + ¾" [1.9cm]).

7 Fold one of the strips in half lengthwise, with the wrong sides together, and press the fold with an iron.

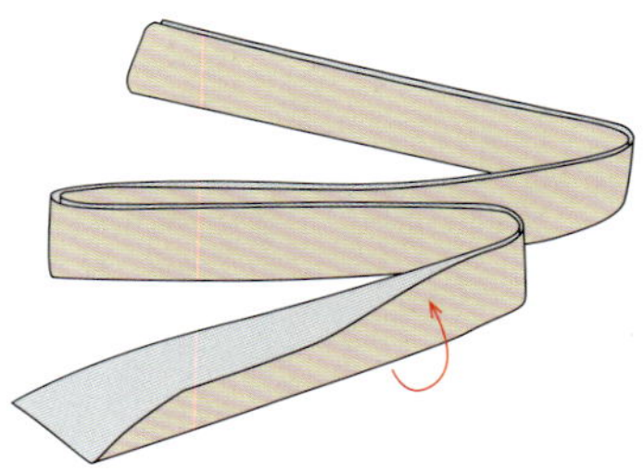

8 Pin the band to the bottom of one sleeve, with right sides together. Once the strip has been folded over the edge, make sure the center fold is directly above the edge of the cuff. The two ends that extend ⅜" (1cm) beyond the edges of the sleeve should be folded over to the wrong side. Stitch around ⅜" (1cm) from the edge of the strip.

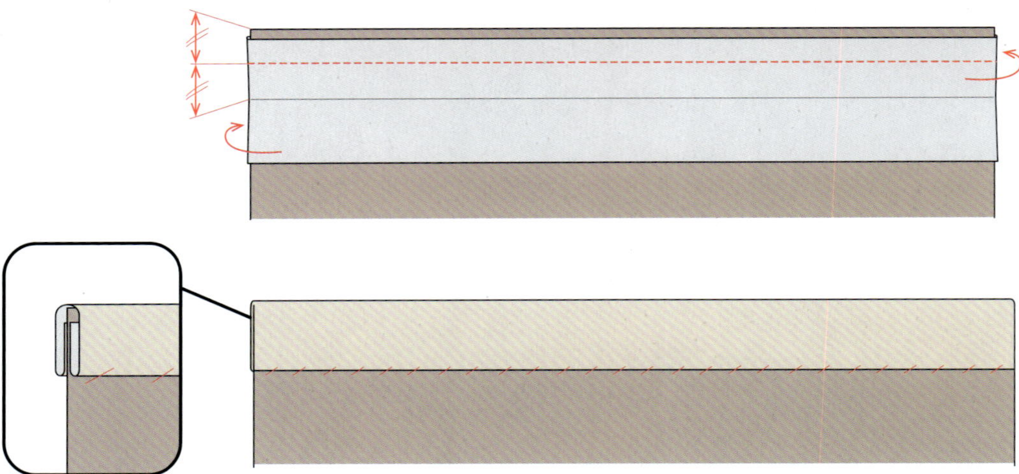

9 Fold the strip over to the inside. The center crease will run around the bottom of the sleeve. Turn up ¼" (6.4mm) along the free edge and pin in place. Baste and sew with blind stitches.

ELBOW PATCHES

10 Trace the Elbow Pad Template onto a sheet of acetate. Trace and cut two pieces, using different wool fabrics.

11 Place the elbow pads on the sleeves. Embroider around the edges using straight or blanket stitches.

SMALL APPLIQUÉS

12 Cut small squares or rectangles of different sizes from various scraps of wool fabric. Place them on the jacket. Baste, then embroider around the edges using a running stitch.

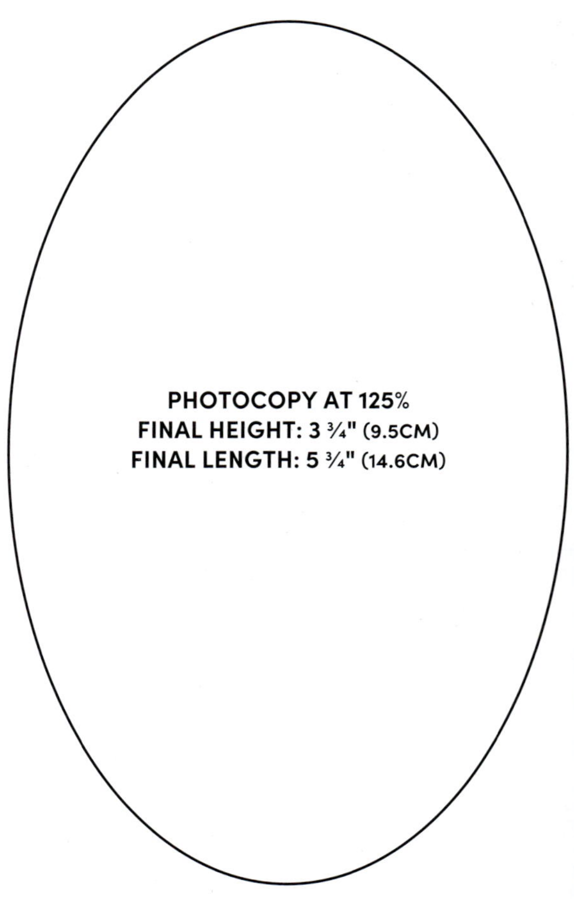

The nice thing about this project is that it presents so many design elements that you can pick and choose from. You might want to just add the lapels and elbow pads, and that's fine! Customize your clothing all you like.

Quilt Block Corduroy Jacket

A few scraps of denim pieced together give a corduroy jacket a cool new look.

TECHNIQUES

- Piecing, traditional appliqué, and embroidery
- *See pages 9, 15, and 20.*

MATERIALS

- Acetate sheet
- Scraps of denim fabric
- Heat-erasable pen or tailor's chalk
- Matching sewing threads
- Corduroy jacket
- Embroidery threads

The instructions are for pockets measuring 7½" (19.1cm) wide. If your jacket has different pockets, adjust the dimensions of Square A.

QUILT BLOCKS

1 Trace Templates A, B, and C onto a sheet of acetate (see page 87). To make one block, cut from scraps of denim:

- 1 Square A
- 4 Square B
- 1 Square C

Tip: This quick technique allows you to make the block without making triangles or octagons. Sewing diagonally across the squares will prevent the finished triangle from becoming distorted. The leftovers can be used for other small projects or added to your scrap bag.

2 Using an erasable pen or chalk, draw a diagonal line from corner to corner on the wrong side of the four B squares. Place one Square B at each corner of Square A, right sides together. Stitch across the marked diagonal.

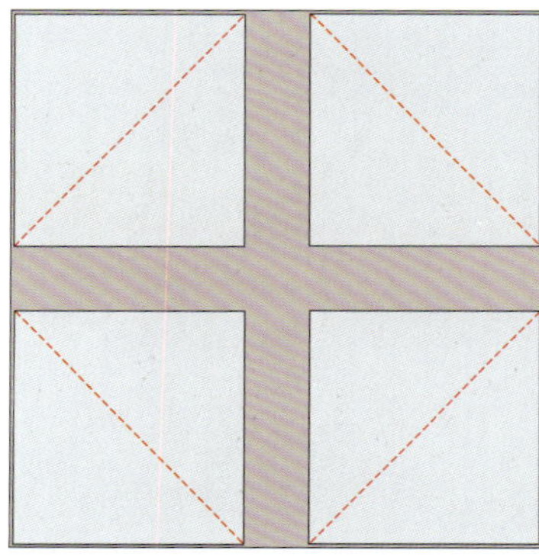

3 Cut off the excess from the B squares, ¼" (6.4mm) away from the seam. Be careful not to cut through the fabric underneath.

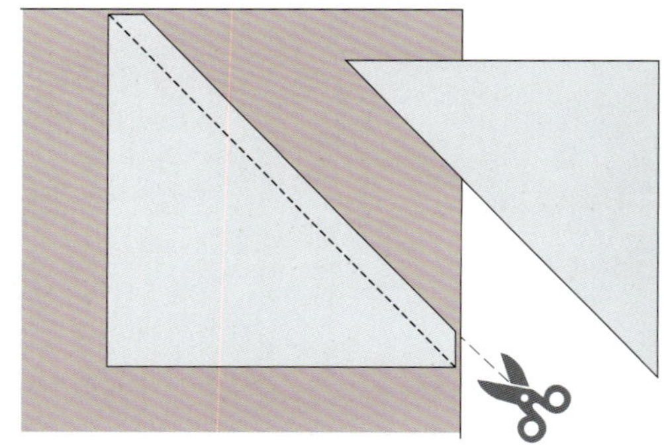

This pocket detail can be swapped out with any quilt block. Either design your own or look up options online to find one that appeals to you.

4 Fold the B triangles toward the outer edge of A so that they cover the seam allowance, and press with an iron.

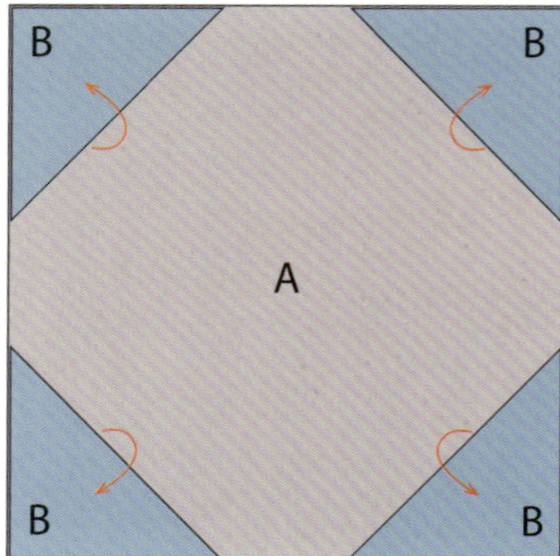

5 Turn a ¼" (6.4mm) hem all the way around Square C and baste. Place it in the center of Square A, rotating it 45 degrees. Pin and baste. Make small slip stitches all the way around.

6 Turn under a small hem all the way around Square A and place it on the pocket. Pin and baste. Make small slip stitches all the way around the block.

7 Make the other pocket in the same way.

8 Embroider running stitches around the inside of the various pieces that make up the block.

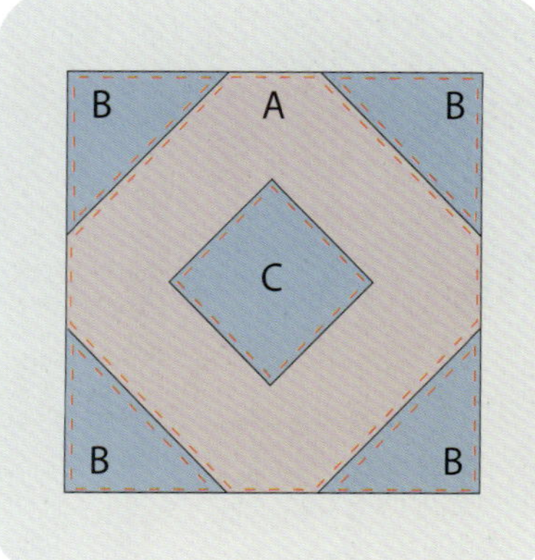

FINISHING TOUCHES

9 Remove all the basting stitches.

10 Embroider the edges of the jacket and the bottom of the sleeves using the blanket stitch.

This pocket detail can be swapped out with any quilt block. Either design your own or look up options online to find one that appeals to you.

7 ¼"
(18.4cm)
7 ¼"
(18.4cm)
PHOTOCOPY AT 135 %
A

3 ⅛"
(7.9cm)
B
3 ⅛"
(7.9cm)
PHOTOCOPY AT 135 %

3"
(7.6cm)
C
3"
(7.6cm)
PHOTOCOPY AT 133 %

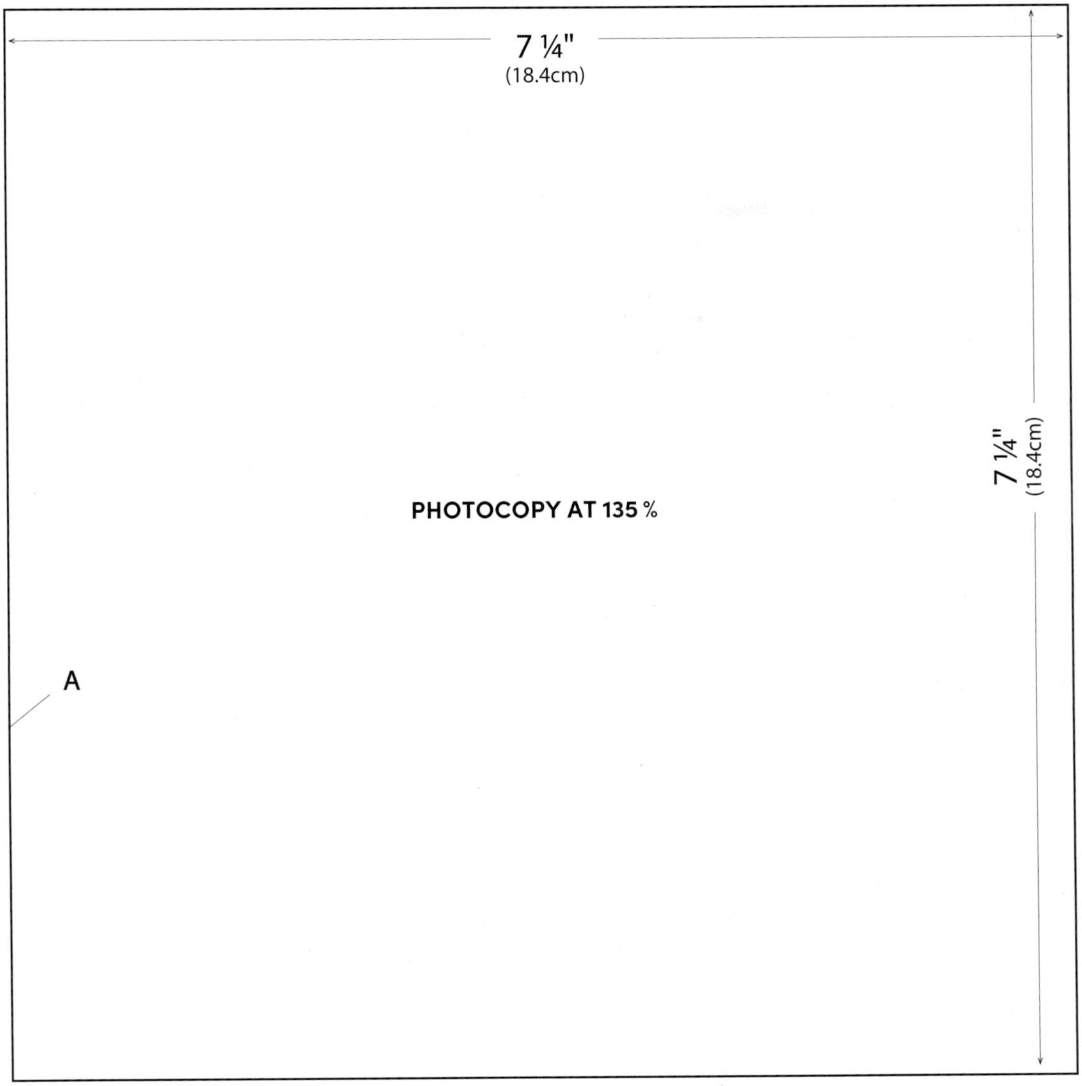

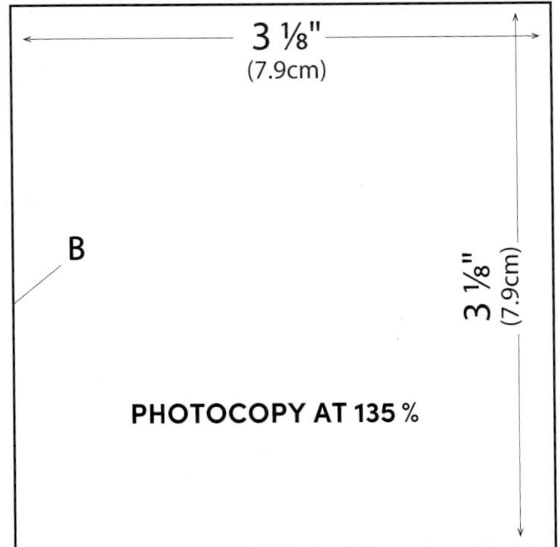

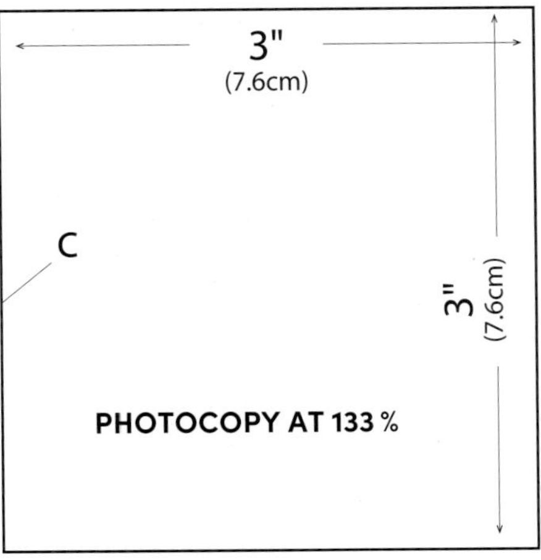

Geometric Appliqué Jacket

Pieces of fabric cut into different shapes and sizes are placed here and there on a classic jacket, giving it a fresh new look.

TECHNIQUES

- Traditional appliqué and embroidery
- *See pages 15 and 20.*

MATERIALS

- Scraps of solid fabric
- Wool jacket
- Matching sewing threads
- Heat-erasable pen
- Embroidery threads

1 Cut out pieces of fabric in different shapes, sizes, and colors.

2 Turn a ¼" (6.4mm) hem to the wrong side, and follow the traditional appliqué technique (page 15).

3 Position the motifs on the jacket front and sleeves as desired. Baste in place.

4 Sew small slip stitches around the edges using thread that matches the fabric.

5 Remove the basting stitches.

6 Using an erasable pen, draw lines on the jacket to connect the base fabric and the appliqué pieces. Embroider the lines with running stitches. Erase the marks.

The appliquéd pieces might look disjointed on their own, so the embroidered stitches ties everything together and makes the design look intentional.

Patchwork Denim Jacket

This denim jacket really makes a statement with its print fabric detailing.

TECHNIQUE

- Traditional appliqué
- *See page 15.*

MATERIALS

- Scraps of print fabric
- Matching threads
- Denim jacket

RIGHT FRONT

1 Cut two pieces of fabric measuring 3⅛" x 9" (7.9 x 22.9cm) and 2" x 2¼" (5.1 x 5.7cm). Turn a ¼" (6.4mm) hem all the way around each piece and baste.

2 Place the small rectangle on top of the large one, pin in place, and baste. Machine stitch all around with a matching thread.

3 Place the unit on the Right Front (as shown in the opposite page inset), pin, and baste. Machine stitch.

4 Remove the basting stitches.

LEFT FRONT

5 Cut two pieces of fabric measuring 3¾" x 5¼" (9.5 x 13.3cm) and 3⅜" x 3½" (8.6 x 8.9cm). Turn a ¼" (6.4mm) hem all the way around each piece and baste.

6 Place the two rectangles on the Left Front (as shown right) near the top, overlapping them slightly. Pin and baste. Machine stitch.

7 Remove the basting stitches.

BACK

8 Following the previous instructions, cut and then attach to the back:

- 1 rectangle, 3¾" x 4⅜" (9.5 x 11.1cm), on the left side
- 2 rectangles, 6¾" x 8½" (17.1 x 21.6cm) and 3¼" x 3½" (8.3 x 8.9cm), at the top, layered
- 1 square, 4¾" x 4¾" (12.1 x 12.1cm), below the previous rectangles, overlapping them slightly
- 1 rectangle, 4⅛" x 8⅝" (10.5 x 21.9cm), at the bottom

This is a great way to show off your favorite prints in your scrap stash, which might not work in any other project.

Jacket with Yo-Yos

Colorful fabric circles brighten up a classic jacket.

TECHNIQUE
- Yo-yo
- *See page 13.*

MATERIALS
- Acetate sheet
- Scraps of fabric in different colors
- Matching threads
- Cotton jacket

1 Two sizes of yo-yos have been used here, using Template A and Template B. Trace both onto a sheet of acetate.

2 Make around 30 yo-yos using Template A and 12 yo-yos using Template B following the technique (page 13).

FRONT

3 Position the yo-yos on one side of the front, along the placket, alternating A and B yo-yos. You can also place a B on top of an A.

4 Baste, then secure with small running stitches using matching thread.

CUFFS

5 Place A yo-yos around the bottom of the sleeves, spacing them about ¼" (6.4mm) apart. Secure them as before.

COLLAR

6 Join two B yoyos to the tops of two A yoyos. Place them on the tips of the collar. Secure them as before.

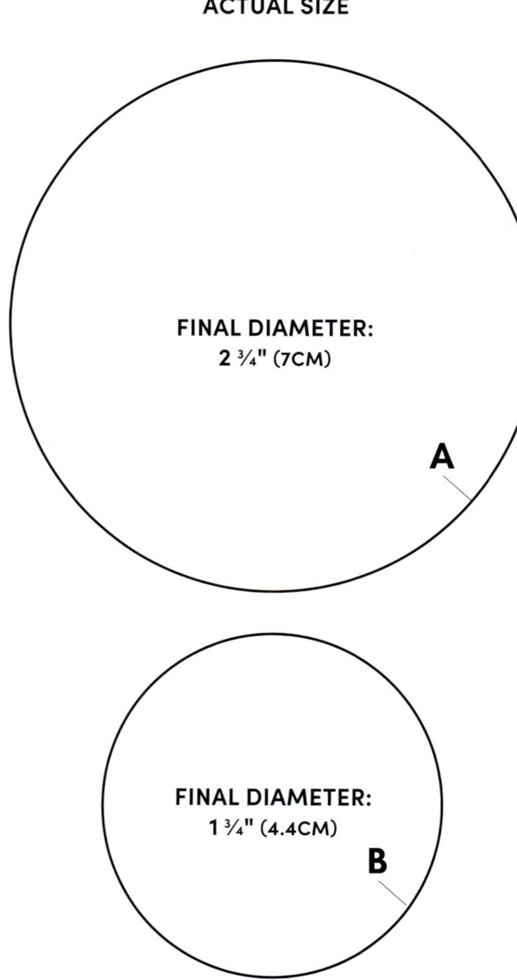

BERGAMOT &
JASMINE
Je t'aime

Boro Denim Jacket

Squares and rectangles of different sizes, cut from denim and embroidered, rescue this shabby shirt jacket.

TECHNIQUE

- Boro
- *See page 14.*

MATERIALS

- Scraps of denim fabric
- Long denim shirt or jacket
- Embroidery threads

1 Cut out squares and rectangles of various sizes from scraps of denim.

2 Place them on the front of the jacket. Try a few combinations until you get the look you want. Some pieces can overlap or layer on top of each other.

3 Baste all the pieces to the jacket.

4 Sew around the edges using large running stitches in embroidery thread.

5 Remove the basting stitches.

Keeping the appliqués monotone by using different shades of blue lends a classy look to the revamped design.

Cosabeth Parriaud is a well-known name in the quilt world as a designer, teacher, artist, and author. She creates designs for specialist magazines and textile publications. Upcycling and repurposing textiles have been her passion for many years. She also teaches on Artesane.com and gives classes on various patchwork-related topics in France and throughout Europe.

Best known for her work with color and transparency, she has been involved in the contemporary patchwork movement since its inception, and her quilts have been featured in major exhibitions in France and abroad.

Cosabeth is the author of the book *Le Patchwork*, published by Marabout in 2022. She is also the coauthor of three other books: *Les Patchworks du Rouvray* (Martingale/T.P.P), *Patchwork, Les bases* (LTA), and *Provence, Quilts and Cuisine*, published by C&T in English.

ACKNOWLEDGMENTS

- My warmest thanks to Éditions Marie-Claire for their confidence in me.
- Thank you to my editor, Isabelle Misery, for her invaluable support.
- Thank you to Corinne Jamet for the photos and to Vania Leroy-Thuillier for the design.
- Thank you to my sons, Alexandre and Mathieu Marziou, and to my daughters-in-law, Anne-Sophie Krissi and Anna Lachkar, for being such wonderful models in this book. I am also grateful for their wise advice regarding my commitment to upcycling.
- Thank you to my husband, Yves Marziou, for his encouragement and support.
- Thank you to the Maison Caillebotte in Yerres (91330) for their warm welcome during the photoshoot.